Achieving

QTS

The 2012 Teachers' Standards in the Classroom

9/2013

The 2012 Teachers' Standards in the Classroom

Roy Blatchford

Los Angeles | London | New Delhi
Singapore | Washington DC

Learning Matters
An imprint of SAGE Publications Ltd
1 Oliver's Yard
55 City Road
London EC1Y 1SP

SAGE Publications Inc.
2455 Teller Road
Thousand Oaks, California 91320

SAGE Publications India Pvt Ltd
B 1/I 1 Mohan Cooperative Industrial
Area
Mathura Road
New Delhi 110 044

SAGE Publications Asia-Pacific Pte Ltd
3 Church Street
#10-04 Samsung Hub
Singapore 049483

Editor: Amy Thornton
Production controller: Chris Marke
Project management: Deer Park
Productions, Tavistock, Devon
Marketing manager: Catherine Slinn
Cover design: Toucan design
Typeset by: PDQ Typesetting Ltd
Printed and bound in Great Britain by:
MPG Books Group, Bodmin, Cornwall

British Library Cataloguing in Publication
data

A catalogue record for this book is
available from the British Library

ISBN 978-1-44625-634-3 (pbk)
ISBN 978-1-44625 633-6

MIX
Paper from
responsible sources
FSC
www.fsc.org   FSC® C018575

Contents

Acknowledgements

The Teachers' Standards are © Crown copyright 2011.

You may re-use the information in the Teachers' Standards (excluding logos) free of charge in any format or medium, under the terms of the Open Government Licence. To view this licence, visit www.nationalarchives.gov.uk/doc/open-government-licence/ or e-mail: psi@nationalarchives.gsi.gov.uk

The publication is also available for download at www.education.gov.uk

About the author

Roy Blatchford is Director of the National Education Trust (www.nationaleducationtrust.net).

Previously he was Her Majesty's Inspector of Schools (HMI) in England, with lead responsibilities for school improvement and for the national inspection of good and outstanding schools. Roy has extensive experience of writing inspection frameworks, nationally and internationally, and has inspected and reviewed over 800 schools and colleges in the UK and Europe, USA, Middle East and India.

Roy was Principal of Walton High and Walton Learning Centre in Milton Keynes, opened in September 1999 and described by OFSTED as 'a first class centre of learning – innovative and inspiring'. He was Founding Director (1996–1998) of Reading Is Fundamental, UK, a non-profit organisation developing children's reading and family literacy. From 1986–1996 he was Headteacher of Bicester Community College, an Oxfordshire comprehensive school serving 1200+ 11–19 year old students.

He spent 12 years teaching in inner-London schools, youth and adult services, and has for 30 years been a trainer and speaker with schools, parents, governors and local authorities on literacy, raising student achievement, curriculum development, school improvement, leadership and innovation. He has served as an adviser to various governments, most recently as Deputy Chair/Chair of Drafting Group of the DfE Teachers' Standards Review.

Roy has worked with HM Prison Service, the NHS and the Arts Council in a number of voluntary capacities, and is a visiting Fellow at Oxford Brookes University. He is the author/editor of over 150 books and is a regular contributor to the national media.

Who is this book for?
How is it organised?

The 2012 Teachers' Standards in the Classroom is aimed primarily at those training to teach, in whatever setting. Just as the Standards themselves are addressed to classrooms in primary, special and secondary schools, so is the intent of this book. Whether you are training to teach early years' children, lower secondary pupils or sixth form students, the book should offer something by way of information, reflection, advice and inspiration.

Equally, it is intended that the content will speak with relevance to teachers who are already qualified and experienced, and who are seeking to refresh their own professional development in the light of what will for them be newly expressed standards and expectations.

Teaching is quite simply one of the best jobs in the world, for the many, many who enjoy it. For that small minority of teachers – and sadly you meet a few in staffrooms – who do not enjoy their work or have become tired of its challenges, teaching must be a sad existence, for them and, worryingly, for those they teach. It is a profession to be embraced with both hands, positive spirit, good health, a lively mind, and an unequivocal commitment to young people.

The book follows a straightforward format.

There is an introduction and background section, which gives a context for the Teachers' Standards effective from 1 September 2012. This section concludes with a discussion of the **Preamble** to the actual Standards, a statement of professional intent and aspiration for all teachers to embrace.

Chapters 1 to 8 consider in turn each of the eight key Standards – **Part 1** of the Teachers' Standards document – as set out by the

Department for Education (DfE), examining their content and purpose, and how trainee teachers might be expected to demonstrate, with evidence, that they are meeting the Standards. For those in training settings around the country, whether school or higher education based, the text seeks to complement the expert guidance afforded by tutors and their own supporting materials.

Chapter 9 focuses on **Part 2** of the Standards, unambiguously titled 'Personal and Professional Conduct', and applicable to all who teach in the nation's schools, whatever their position or length of service within the teaching profession.

Chapter 10 is entitled 'Master Teacher'. Why? In establishing the Teachers' Standards, the DfE invited the group writing the Standards to create a further set of draft criteria describing what might be the qualities and distinguishing features of high performing teachers. This Master Teacher Standard is included here by way of 'extension material' for interested readers, and may be of keen interest to experienced teachers within the profession. (At the time of this book's publication, the DfE had made no formal decision as to the wider use of the term 'Master Teacher' within the teaching profession.)

Chapter 11 presents important detail from the Ofsted *School Inspection Handbook* (Ofsted, 2012a), and how Ofsted inspectors judge the quality of teaching and learning in classrooms. Further, it examines how the Teachers' Standards and the Ofsted criteria compare.

Chapter 12 presents a wider perspective on successful schools. Fulfilled and confident teachers deserve to be well led by those who believe in an aspirational culture, and to work in schools which are both restless to improve and consistently outward-facing.

Chapter 13 brings together articles and recommended further reading: stories and accounts to remind you that teaching is a noble profession, with incident, routine, humour, alarums and moments of sheer elation.

And there are three 'Interludes' which punctuate the book. Each of these is presented as a series of questions to ask yourself when entering classrooms across the 3–18 age range in search of good and excellent practice. They are rooted in the author's own observations of more than 8,000 lessons all around the world over the past decade. The more experienced you become in a classroom, the more you are able to ask these questions intuitively.

Finally, a few house style points.

- **As formally set out by the DfE, each of the Teachers' Standards has its own heading, followed by a number of bulleted sub-headings. The bullets, which are an integral part of the Standards, are designed to *amplify the scope of each heading*. For ease of reference in this book, the bullets have been identified by letters, from A to E. Good teaching, by its very nature, is a distinctive cocktail of skills and techniques, so readers will inevitably find some sub-headings across the standards complementing and reinforcing one another.**
- **To help the reader interrogate the Standards, and other parts of the book, analysis and advice are presented under three headings: *Commentary* – offers pointers as to how teachers may interpret the Standards in their everyday practice; *Reflections* – seeks to develop the good habits of the 'reflective practioner'; these could be used as starters for group discussion in a training context; *Evidence* – for the trainee teacher, suggestions about providing evidence against the Standards to a tutor mentor, whether they are visiting the trainee in the classroom, or viewing an online portfolio, or during a group session at the training institution.**
- **The term 'classroom' has been used throughout the book. It is used in the generic sense, to include workshops, laboratories, gymnasia, sports fields and outdoor settings, dance studios, music practice rooms and any space where teachers may find themselves leading young minds.**

- The word 'pupils' is taken to include children, learners, students, whatever the reader's preferred term might be, given his or her individual teaching setting.
- When referring to an individual teacher or pupil, licence has sometimes been taken with accompanying singulars and plurals; for example, the grammatically incorrect 'they' is used rather than the potentially clumsy 'he/she'. This goes against my purist instincts, but is a stylistic imperfection which I hope the reader can live with in this context.

Roy Blatchford
Oxford 2013

Introduction to the Teachers' Standards

Background

September 2012 saw the introduction of new Teachers' Standards which replaced the existing qualified teacher status (QTS) and Core Standards, and the GTCE's Code of Practice for Registered Teachers in England. The new Standards set out the minimum requirements for teachers' professional practice and conduct. Teachers' performance is to be assessed against them as part of the appraisal arrangements for schools.

In drawing up the standards during 2011, the Independent Review of Teachers' Standards was given the remit to develop new standards of competence, ethics and behaviour which reflect the trust and professionalism society should expect from its teachers (DfE, 2011a). To that end, the new Standards begin with a Preamble, a founding statement of expectations:

> *Teachers make the education of their pupils their first concern, and are accountable for achieving the highest possible standards in work and conduct. Teachers act with honesty and integrity; have strong subject knowledge, keep their knowledge and skills as teachers up-to-date and are self-critical; forge positive professional relationships; and work with parents in the best interests of their pupils.*
>
> (DfE, 2012a, p7)

What happens in classrooms

On a personal note, I have had the great privilege during the past decade to observe over 8,000 classrooms, from Mumbai to New York, Barcelona to Birmingham, Jeddah to Jarrow. At their best, these are the vibrant classrooms which teachers create because they are spending many of their waking hours within them. They are the places where young minds flourish. These sparkling classrooms are places and atmospheres which remain long in the minds and spirits of the learners.

When I joined HMI in 2004, David Bell HMCI advised me to reflect on the wisdom of a previous chief inspector, Martin Roseveare: 'You should remember that when you visit a school it is an everyday affair for you, but an unusual and important occasion for the school'. I remind myself of those words every day I sign in to a school's visitors' book.

In the academic year 2011–12 I observed over 700 lessons, as part of the National Education Trust's school improvement services (www.nationaleducationtrust.net). Special, primary, secondary, state and independent, home and abroad – schools have welcomed me with warm hospitality and in the spirit of championing what is great, recognising what is good, and suggesting a few even-better-ifs.

What did I learn during that year in classrooms?

- **That childhood is safe in the nation's primary schools.**
- **That in socially challenging schools, the teachers have to run just for the pupils to stand still.**
- **That great lessons are all about richness of task, rooted in teachers' excellent subject knowledge and passion to share that knowledge with students.**
- **That pupils' prior knowledge of a subject is endlessly surprising.**
- **That, in the best classrooms, IT is used like a pair of scissors, no more no less.**
- **That skilled early years' practitioners have much to teach everyone else about the power of timely digression and intervention.**
- **That teachers spend hours marking, but too often pupils don't do justice to that marking.**
- **That doing more of the same is not going to transform standards of attainment – doing *differently* can.**
- **That teachers may cry when you tell them they have taught a great lesson.**
- **That the best teachers are children at heart.**
- **That sitting in the best lessons, you just don't want to leave . . .**

In the best schools I visit there is a central paradox which runs through them like Brighton through a stick of rock. It is this: the schools are at one and the same time very secure in their values and ways of doing, yet simultaneously restless to improve.

So too with the sparkling classroom practitioner, who is absolutely in the grip of well tried, tested and effective practices yet simultaneously questing to improve their teaching of a particular topic or skill. Show me the teacher who asks at the end of a day: what have I learned as a teacher today? What shall I do (a) the same and (b) differently next time?

What the Teachers' Standards 2012 say

The Review considered a wide range of international and national evidence, including evidence submitted by key users of standards before developing the Teachers' Standards. The new Standards had to provide a benchmark of the minimum requirements that should be expected of trainees and teachers.

In essence, the Standards had to raise the bar and highlight the characteristics of good teaching. Above all, the Standards needed to be clear, simple and assessable, and identify the key elements of teaching, and the expectations of professional conduct that underpin the practice of teachers at all career stages.

The Review was clear, however, that the Standards should not define the award of QTS and the end of a teacher's induction period as two separate career stages, principally because the induction period should be about consolidating ITT and demonstrating consistency of practice. Trainees and teachers should demonstrate that they meet all of the Standards, which define the level of practice at which all qualified teachers should be expected to perform.

The new Standards do not prescribe in detail what good or outstanding teaching looks like; this should be determined by ITT providers, headteachers and teachers, using their professional judgement as relevant to context, roles and responsibilities. The new Standards should assist them in making such decisions by providing a clear framework within which such judgements can be made.

The Review also recommended that the Post-Threshold, Excellent Teacher and Advanced Skills Teacher standards should be discontinued, and advocated the introduction of a Master Teacher Standard (see Chapter 10, and DfE, 2011b). This Standard is made up of five core domains (modelled on international best practice) within which very good teachers can demonstrate their abilities:

1.   Knowledge

2.   Classroom Performance

3.   Outcomes

4.   Environment and Ethos

5.   Professional Context

The Secretary of State is considering these recommendations and will respond in due course. In the meantime, the existing higher-level standards continue to apply.

It is the Review Group's view that the new Teachers' Standards, and the proposed new Master Teacher Standard, will provide a new progressive career framework for teachers that will both raise the prestige of the profession, and improve teacher quality.

From my personal standpoint, the Teachers' Standards 2012 are a once-in-a-generation opportunity for teachers across the country to unite behind a set of professional expectations which are focused unequivocally on the classroom. If all teachers meet these expectations we shall have a profession of which society can be rightly proud.

Key quotations from the Teachers' Standards 2012 document

The Teachers' Standards 2012 are published in a self-contained eight-page document which should be read by all teachers (DfE, 2012a). The following list of key quotations is particularly relevant to trainee teachers. The source of each quotation is indicated.

> *The new standards will apply to the vast majority of teachers regardless of their career stage. The Teachers' Standards will apply to: trainees working towards QTS; all teachers completing their statutory induction period; and those covered by the new performance appraisal arrangements.*
>
> (para 3, p2)

> *The new standards define the minimum level of practice expected of trainees and teachers from the point of being awarded QTS.*
>
> (para 5, p2)

> *The new standards will need to be applied as appropriate to the role and context within which a trainee or teacher is practising. Providers of initial teacher training (ITT) will assess trainees against the standards in a way that is consistent with what could reasonably be expected of a trainee teacher prior to the award of QTS.*
>
> (para 6, p3)

> *Headteachers (or appraisers) will assess qualified teachers against the standards to a level that is consistent with what should reasonably be expected of a teacher in the relevant role and at the relevant stage of their career.*
>
> (para 7, p3)

The new standards are presented as separate headings, numbered 1 to 8, each of which is accompanied by a number of bulleted sub-headings. The bullets, which are an integral part of the standards, are designed to amplify the scope of each heading.

(para 13, p4)

The bulleted sub-headings should not be interpreted as separate standards in their own right, but should be used by those assessing trainees and teachers to track progress against the standard, to determine areas where additional development might need to be observed, or to identify areas where a trainee or teacher is already demonstrating excellent practice to that standard.

(para 13, p4)

Appropriate self-evaluation, reflection and professional development activity is critical to improving teachers' practice at all career stages. The standards set out clearly the key areas in which a teacher should be able to assess his or her own practice, and receive feedback from colleagues.

(para 14, p4)

As their careers progress, teachers will be expected to extend the depth and breadth of knowledge, skill and understanding that they demonstrate in meeting the standards, as is judged appropriate to the role they are fulfilling and the context in which they are working.

(para 14, p4)

REFLECTIONS

1. Make sure you have a clear understanding of these key quotations, and how they apply to your first year in teaching.

    What record-keeping are you developing to ensure you are:

    (a) tracking progress against the Standards

(b) determining areas for development

(c) identifying your best practice?

2. What systems are securely in place to ensure you have prompt and timely feedback on all aspects of your developing practice?

3. Are you clear about the 'sign-off' procedures relating to your meeting of the Standards?

The Preamble to the Standards

PREAMBLE

Teachers make the education of their pupils their first concern, and are accountable for achieving the highest possible standards in work and conduct. Teachers act with honesty and integrity; have strong subject knowledge, keep their knowledge and skills as teachers up-to-date and are self-critical; forge positive professional relationships; and work with parents in the best interests of their pupils.

(DfE, 2012a, p7)

The Preamble summarises the values and behaviour that all teachers must demonstrate throughout their careers. At one level it is perhaps a statement of the obvious, and such a description has not previously been applied to the teaching profession in this country.

Yet preambles such as this are no stranger to other professions. They have long been an integral part of conditions of service for doctors, lawyers, accountants, architects and others.

By way of comparison, the reader may be interested to glance over the following, drawn from different professions, and reflect on the various expectations which are set down, for the trainee and the experienced professional alike.

Lawyers

In a society founded on respect for the rule of law the lawyer fulfils a special role. His duties do not begin and end with the faithful performance of what he is instructed to do so far as the law permits. A lawyer must serve the interests of justice as well as those whose rights and liberties he is trusted to assert and defend, and it is his duty not only to plead his client's cause but to be his adviser.

A lawyer's function therefore lays on him a variety of legal and moral obligations (sometimes appearing to be in conflict with each other) towards:

- *the client;*
- *the courts and other authorities before whom the lawyer pleads his client's cause or acts on his behalf;*
- *the legal profession in general and each fellow member of it in particular;*
- *the public for whom the existence of a free and independent profession, bound together by respect for rules made by the profession itself, is an essential means of safeguarding human rights in face of the power of the state and other interests in society.*

(from the European Lawyers Code of Conduct,
www.barstandardsboard.org.uk)

Architects

You are expected at all times to act with honesty and integrity and to avoid any actions or situations which are inconsistent with your professional obligations. This standard underpins the Code and will be taken to be required in any consideration of your conduct under any of the other standards.

You should not make any statement which is contrary to your professional opinion or which you know to be misleading, unfair to others or discreditable to the profession.

Where a conflict of interest arises you are expected to disclose it in writing and manage it to the satisfaction of all affected parties. You should seek written confirmation that all parties involved give their informed consent to your continuing to act. Where this consent is not received you should cease acting for one or more of the parties.

Where you make or receive any payment or other inducement for the introduction or referral of work, you should disclose the arrangement to the client or prospective client at the outset.

(from the Architects Registration Board code of conduct, www.arb.org.uk/professional_standards)

Doctors

Patients need good doctors. Good doctors make the care of their patients their first concern: they are competent, keep their knowledge and skills up to date, establish and maintain good relationships with patients and colleagues, are honest and trustworthy, and act with integrity.

(from *Good Medical Practice,* General Medical Council, 2012, www.gmc-uk.org/guidance/good_medical_practice)

REFLECTIONS

1. In what ways are the above similar and different in their expectations and values?
2. How do they compare in content with the Preamble to the Teachers' Standards?
3. Is there anything you would amend about the Preamble to the Teachers' Standards?

1
Set high expectations which inspire, motivate and challenge pupils

1 **A teacher must: set high expectations which inspire, motivate and challenge pupils**

A establish a safe and stimulating environment for pupils, rooted in mutual respect

B set goals that stretch and challenge pupils of all backgrounds, abilities and dispositions

C demonstrate consistently the positive attitudes, values and behaviour which are expected of pupils.

(DfE, 2012a, p7)

COMMENTARY > > > > > > COMMENTARY > > > > > >

The cornerstone of effective teaching lies in the expectations teachers set down for their pupils. Hence, the Teachers' Standards begin – Standard 1 – with expecting all teachers to set high expectations which inspire, motivate and challenge pupils. All three verbs are equally important, though each of them will quite properly be interpreted differently by the teacher of a Reception class or an A-level economics group.

In amplifying the scope of the Standard 1 heading, there are three stated areas for teachers to focus upon.

A   Safety is non-negotiable, and this will take on a different dimension if the teacher is at work on a school playing field, in a drama studio or in a science laboratory. The environment itself needs to stimulate the learner, and that may be through wall display or the exhibiting of artefacts relevant to the subject under study. And the whole culture of the classroom must of course promote a learning climate within which pupils and adults treat one another with dignity and where mutual respect is of the essence.

B   By their very nature, all classrooms contain a population of unique individuals, including the teacher and any support staff. The teacher must set significant store by, and invest time in, getting to know those they teach. Not only do pupils come from different family backgrounds, creeds and cultures. Abilities and dispositions vary, often significantly, as do aspirations and pupils' own self-esteem. Once the teacher knows the distinctive characteristics and characters of the pupils, they are then in a strong position to ensure that lessons are planned and delivered in a way that ensures all pupils are challenged and stretched.

C   Pupils will always mirror their teachers' attitudes and behaviour. This is as true of seven year olds in an infant classroom as it is true of a GCSE class of teenagers. Where a teacher is negative and indulges in the 'dark sarcasm of the classroom', pupils will surely be infected by such an approach. Where a teacher is consistently upbeat and can-do, the class will catch the same mood. The teacher's positive values, warmly shared, complemented by their own modelling of good behaviours, have a decisive impact on the well-being and fruitful commerce of the classroom.

REFLECTIONS

1. Think of a classroom you have visited which immediately grabbed your attention and evoked a very positive emotional response. What were its constituent features by way of physical organisation and 'feel'?

2. Think of a classroom you have visited which gave out the opposite impressions. What were its constituent features?

3. Which techniques have you observed amongst experienced teachers for getting to know pupils quickly and intelligently?

4. Think of a lesson you have seen where the teacher was clearly able to challenge the intellectual thinking of all pupils. How did they do this effectively?

5. From observing fellow professionals, we learn what *not* to do as well as what to do. Reflect on the everyday classroom practice of a teacher you have seen whose values and positive classroom beha-viours you would wish to emulate.

EVIDENCE EVIDENCE **EVIDENCE** EVIDENCE **EVIDENCE** EVIDENCE

Demonstrate evidence to your tutor mentor of:

- a safe and welcoming physical environment;
- stimulating subject-related displays of pupils' work;
- your strong knowledge of each pupil's abilities and dispositions;
- high expectations permeating classroom practice;
- your positive verbal and body language towards the pupils;
- a clear set of shared values, rooted in mutual respect.

2
Promote good progress and outcomes by pupils

2 A teacher must: promote good progress and outcomes by pupils

A be accountable for pupils' attainment, progress and outcomes

B be aware of pupils' capabilities and prior knowledge and plan teaching to build on these

C guide pupils to reflect on the progress they have made and their emerging needs

D demonstrate knowledge and understanding of how pupils learn and how this impacts on teaching

E encourage pupils to take a responsible and conscientious attitude to their own work and study.

(DfE, 2012a, p7)

COMMENTARY > > > > > > COMMENTARY > > > > > >

Schools exist first and foremost to serve the educational needs of their pupils. Rightly, schools are judged by parents and the wider community on their track-record in (a) how pupils make progress in their various subjects, and (b) the final examination grades and other awards they achieve. It is also fair to say that society at large judges the wider school system on how well it is preparing the next generation of healthy, active and participating citizens.

Standard 2 shines a proper spotlight on the expectation that all pupils should make good progress and enjoy good outcomes during their compulsory school years.

In amplifying the scope of the Standard 2 heading, there are five stated areas for teachers to focus upon.

A The lead adjective here is accountable. As professionals, teachers are fundamentally accountable for what happens in their classrooms. They are accountable to the pupils they teach, to the parents of those pupils, and, usually through line management systems, to the leadership of the school. *What* are teachers accountable for? First on the list is what a pupil attains, that is, academic attainment as measured by tests and examinations. Today's teacher must have a sure command of the school's and pupils' performance data. Second, there is the academic progress a pupil makes over time with the teacher. Third, there are the broader outcomes which, depending on setting, may be measured through aspects of social, emotional and physical development.

B   Standard 1 highlights the vital importance of a teacher knowing the abilities and dispositions of pupils in their class. Building on this base, teachers will come to identify individual pupils' capabilities. Critically, it is vital to identify also what prior knowledge of a subject or skill a pupil already possesses. Failure to do this means pupils will make limited progress. Armed with a thorough knowledge of all the pupils in a class-room, effective lesson planning and harnessing of suitable resources can take place.

C   Teaching and learning are a great double act. One requires the other. The effective teacher helps pupils, through various techniques, to think about the progress they are making, daily, weekly, and over a term or a year. The teacher and pupil reflecting on progress together, through mark-ing and dialogue, identify next steps in learning and what particular support or extension might be required to ensure the pupil's individual needs are met. This is as true of an infant teacher observing the development of fine motor skills, as it is of the GCSE history teacher concentrating on improving essay writing skills with their group.

D   In the same way that a hand surgeon needs to have detailed knowl-edge of the nerves, tendons and arteries of that part of the body, so the professional teacher needs excellent technical background know-how. The primary specialist will have a clear understanding of cognitive development in say, seven year-olds, and how teaching approaches need to be adjusted to secure effective progress in mathematics in a Year 2 classroom. Equally, the A-level teacher of economics will bring to their seminar group a secure command of the impact of different study skills and analytics, so that pupils can be helped to approach a demanding concept from different directions in order to grasp its complexities.

E   Skilful teaching is also about a degree of 'letting go'. The teacher cannot do it all. Consistent with the age and growing maturity of the pupil, the teacher should encourage independence. This independence will be demonstrated by pupils taking a responsible and conscientious approach to their classwork and homework. It will not happen by magic. Effective teachers nudge, cajole and model independent learning habits. Good teachers and good parents have in common that they give 'roots and wings' to their children.

REFLECTIONS

REFLECTIONS

1. What do you understand by the word 'accountable'? In your particular school setting, what lines of accountability are (a) clearly, and (b) less clearly set out?

2. Are you clear as to whom you are accountable, and for what?

3. How does the school in which you work define 'attainment', 'progress' and 'outcomes'? What is your working understanding of these terms?

4. What is your command and working knowledge of (a) the whole school's data, and (b) the performance data for the pupils you teach?

5. What techniques do you plan using to ensure that you have a good grasp of pupils' prior knowledge and capabilities?

6. What have you observed by way of best practice in relation to teachers helping pupils reflect on progress?

7. What particular strengths, knowledge and skills do you have which will enable you to gain a quick understanding of how pupils are learning in your classroom?

8. Think of a teacher from your own school days who helped you become an independent learner. What 'tricks' did they use? How will you successfully promote responsible attitudes to work among the pupils you teach? How might you approach the pupil who is resistant to taking responsibility for his or her own learning?

EVIDENCE EVIDENCE **EVIDENCE** EVIDENCE **EVIDENCE** EVIDENCE

Demonstrate evidence to your tutor mentor of:

- pupils' attainment in one or two aspects of their learning;

- pupils' progress in another two aspects of learning;

- pupils' outcomes in social, physical or emotional development;

- lesson plans which reflect your strong analysis of pupils' prior knowledge;

- techniques you have used (a) to help pupils reflect on their own progress and (b) to encourage pupils to take responsibility for their own study;

- clear understanding of how pupils are learning effectively in your classroom, and ways in which you have adjusted your teaching to better suit pupils' learning dispositions.

3
Demonstrate good subject and curriculum knowledge

3 A teacher must: demonstrate good subject and curriculum knowledge

A have a secure knowledge of the relevant subject(s) and curriculum areas, foster and maintain pupils' interest in the subject, and address misunderstandings

B demonstrate a critical understanding of developments in the subject and curriculum areas, and promote the value of scholarship

C demonstrate an understanding of and take responsibility for promoting high standards of literacy, articulacy and the correct use of standard English, whatever the teacher's specialist subject

D if teaching early reading, demonstrate a clear understanding of systematic synthetic phonics

E if teaching early mathematics, demonstrate a clear understanding of appropriate teaching strategies.

(DfE, 2012a, pp7–8)

COMMENTARY > > > > > > COMMENTARY > > > > > >

If you ask any pupil what makes a good teacher it is quite likely that the pupil will reply, 'they love their subject'. Indeed, for many teachers, what draws them into the profession is a passion for the subject and a deep interest in children and young people. Standard 3 highlights the fundamental importance of good teaching underpinned by secure knowledge of subject and the wider curriculum.

As in other aspects of the Teachers' Standards, there are self-evident differences when relating this Standard to a particular age group. The teacher of five year-olds needs to demonstrate one kind of command of a range of subjects and topics, combined with a deep understanding of child development. The secondary teacher must demonstrate they have a command of subject which will extend the intellects of pupils from 11–18.

In amplifying the scope of the Standard 3 heading, there are five stated areas for teachers to focus upon.

A   There are three clauses to be noted here. The first pinpoints secure knowledge of subject and curriculum area, a reminder that keeping up to date with the latest developments in a subject is an important tool of the teacher's professionalism. Second, the skilled teacher, building on their knowledge of individual pupils' talents and aptitudes, will introduce ideas and activities that foster new and renewed lines of enquiry. Thirdly, the astute teacher is quick to spot where misunderstandings have occurred, and takes appropriate action to intervene and re-explain a challenging concept or skill.

B   Effective teachers not only keep abreast of the latest developments in their subject, but they are adept at analysing and selecting wisely for classroom use those new techniques, research findings and resources which will have the greatest impact on those they teach. In turn, pupils are quick to recognise those teachers who really know their subject and are able to value and promote 'scholarship'. It is worth commenting that while on the surface we might at first associate the word 'scholarship' with an A-level seminar on 'Othello', the accomplished Year 4 teacher exploring 200 million year-old fossils can soon bring alive the Jurassic coastline of west Dorset in a way that inspires pupils.

C   All teaching and learning is rooted in effective communication. How teachers model the use of language, in all its richness, has a telling impact on young minds. Whatever the teacher's academic background, all who stand before pupils in classrooms have a pivotal responsibility to model and promote high standards in the usage of English. At one level, this requires teachers to think about the specialist keywords of their subject. At another, it means correcting pupils' misuse of grammar in written assignments. And, sensitively carried through with respect for accent and dialect, it means the teacher intervening to ensure that pupils speak clearly and correctly.

There are clearly important training implications for the whole profession within this aspect of Standard 3.

D   The wording here is important: 'if teaching early reading'. At first glance, this appears to be aimed at teachers of younger children. On reflection, it is a stark fact that teachers in the early years of secondary school may also be encountering pupils with faltering reading skills. Whilst many pupils arrive in primary school able to read and demonstrate enjoyment in handling books, a significant minority do not. Those in the profession with responsibilities for early reading must have at their command a secure understanding of the key features and practice of systematic synthetic phonics. They must, for example, have a secure understanding of the importance for beginner readers of grapheme-phoneme correspondence, blending phonemes and segmenting words.

E   An echo of the previous bullet: 'if teaching early mathematics'. While the emphasis in relation to reading is on a particular approach, here the expectation is that teachers will have a secure grasp of a range of suitable teaching techniques when working on mathematics. For example, practical, hands-on experiences of using, comparing and calculating with numbers and quantities and the development of mental methods are of crucial importance in establishing the best mathematical start in primary, up to Year 6. Coupled with this, pupils need plenty of opportunities for developing mathematical language so that they learn to express their thinking using the correct vocabulary.

REFLECTIONS

1. What regular reading and internet researching do you do to ensure that you are up to date with latest developments in the subject and curriculum areas you teach?
2. Which particular techniques and ideas have you harnessed to foster pupils' interest in a subject?
3. Think of an example where you have intervened successfully with a pupil to address a misunderstanding they had about a skill or concept. How did you help the pupil understand, and then move on with confidence to tackle a fresh challenge?

4. What examples have you seen in other teachers' classrooms of materials and ideas which promote real scholarship?

5. What are your own professional strengths when modelling best usage in English, orally and in writing? Do you have any particular training needs?

6. How do you promote articulacy in your own classroom? What expectations do you have when pupils are speaking?

7. For those involved in early reading and mathematics in primary schools: what best practice have you observed and learned from?

8. For those teaching early reading and early mathematics in secondary schools: what best practice have you seen in the special needs department which you might bring to your own classroom?

EVIDENCE EVIDENCE EVIDENCE EVIDENCE EVIDENCE EVIDENCE

Demonstrate evidence to your tutor mentor of:

- recent and relevant background reading, related to your classroom practice;

- classroom displays and/or internet material which reflect topical developments or contemporary issues and debate in your subject;

- examples of materials you have created to foster pupils' interests;

- lesson plans which explicitly reference the 'value of scholarship';

- examples of your marking which focus on pupils' literacy usage;

- where appropriate, classroom practice which demonstrates your ability to teach systematic synthetic phonics and early mathematics with skill and precision.

Interlude: visiting an early years' setting

Read through the following questions which aim to help you reflect on and analyse best practice.

(a) When you visit a colleague's Nursery or Reception classroom, use the following as a checklist against which you observe.

(b) At the end of a given week, use the questions to help you reflect on your own best practice, and where you might wish to fine-tune your own classroom.

(c) Add your own questions to the checklist as you develop your own skills in lesson observations.

The learning environment

1.   Do the outdoor and indoor spaces engage children's interest across all the areas of learning in the revised EYFS?

2.   Does the learning environment provide challenge and extend children's skills and understanding?

3.   Are the furniture and learning resources high quality and in excellent condition?

4.   Is children's work displayed to show it is valued, of high quality, and is diverse?

Relationships

5.   Are children's learning and social needs fully supported by adults?

6.   Are there effective and warm relationships between parents and their child's key person?

7.   Do children have warm and positive relationships with each other? Do they help each other?

Quality of learning

8. Are observations recorded, regularly assessed, and used to inform short term plans?

9. Do staff plan for individual children's next steps of learning, for example in phonics?

10. Are planned activities interesting, inspiring, and appropriate to age and stage of development?

11. Are children provided with achievable challenges and new and exciting activities on offer?

12. Is the daily routine flexible to allow for spontaneous events?

13. Is knowledge of children's preferences and needs used to maximise children's progress?

14. Are individual needs met, e.g. for those with special educational needs, or who are especially talented?

4
Plan and teach well structured lessons

> **4   A teacher must: plan and teach well structured lessons**
>
> A   impart knowledge and develop understanding through effective use of lesson time
>
> B   promote a love of learning and children's intellectual curiosity
>
> C   set homework and plan other out-of-class activities to consolidate and extend the knowledge and understanding pupils have acquired
>
> D   reflect systematically on the effectiveness of lessons and approaches to teaching
>
> E   contribute to the design and provision of an engaging curriculum within the relevant subject area(s).
>
> (DfE, 2012a, p8)

COMMENTARY > > > > > > COMMENTARY > > > > > >

The first three Standards lay out fair and challenging professional foundations: effective teachers possess a love of a subject they know well, combined with an enthusiasm for working with young people; they have consistently high expectations of those they teach; and they expect their pupils to make good progress and outcomes. But how?

Standard 4 shines the spotlight on the craft of the classroom: what is it that is involved in planning and teaching well structured lessons, something that is as important to the teacher in their first year of practice as it is to the senior member of staff in their twentieth year? What is the cocktail of the good lesson?

In amplifying the scope of the Standard 4 heading, there are five stated areas for teachers to focus upon.

A   The teacher, as adult and trained professional, has a body of knowledge to impart. Pupils know and expect this to be the case. Further, pupils look to their teacher to share that knowledge with enthusiasm, passion and a keen eye for what will motivate them. At the heart of learning something new is developing an understanding, to the point where the pupil can teach something they have learned well to someone else. To teach is to learn. Skilled teachers orchestrate lesson time adroitly. They combine their own explanations and interventions with setting aside sufficient time for pupils to explore new ideas and embed understanding. Information technology may play a critical and increasing part here.

B   All classrooms need to be rooted in the fun and fundamentals of learning. Teachers must give their pupils the opportunity to enjoy what they are doing as well as appreciating that mastery of a new topic or skill lies in purposeful practice, occasional failure and 'crying intellectually' before eventual success. The old motto resonates in most classrooms: 'If at first you don't succeed, try, try again'. Good teachers organise their classrooms and lessons in ways which stimulate curious minds, and promote a love of learning for its own sake as well as how that learning can be applied beyond school. This links to the use of the word 'scholarship' in Standard 3.

C   Pupils will tell you that most teachers, from time to time, set homework at the last minute in a lesson because the homework timetable says they must. Good practice lies in lesson planning which integrates classwork and homework wisely so that pupils see the purpose of devoting evening and weekend time to consolidating and extending what they have learned in class. The examination years in secondary school certainly require pupils to be well organised in managing independent study time, so good habits established in primary school are valued by pupils and parents alike.

This bullet point sets further expectations around out-of-class activities, highlighting the importance of school visits and other extra-curricular experiences to enrich the curriculum.

D   In both Standards 2 and 3, teachers are expected to reflect self-critically on practice. It is the hallmark of any good professional: seeking to do something better tomorrow than they did it today. The reflective practitioner is nowhere more important than in this arena of daily practice in the classroom. What did I do today with that high ability maths group which really worked well? Why did I run out of time with that debate activity? What was it about that homework assignment that led to every pupil handing it back to the deadline set? How can I encourage more pupils to present their written work with greater attention to legibility?

E   Whether a trainee teacher or one with many years' experience, you gradually develop a rich bank of tried and tested teaching materials. Many teachers use laptops for lesson planning, sharing what has gone well and less well with colleagues on a daily or weekly basis. Aside from the importance of sharing best practice, this interchange of ideas and materials serves to keep under active revision the curriculum on offer. One of the most exciting aspects of teaching is scrutinising subject content and amending it in the light of experience. Indeed, some teachers get into writing textbooks that way! Teachers new into the profession have much to contribute to ensuring that the curriculum proves engaging and relevant to pupils.

REFLECTIONS

1. What particular personal and professional strengths do you bring to your classroom? Do you have a passion for teaching a particular age range or subject matter?
2. What practice have you seen where a teacher has made skilful use of time? For example, enabling pupils to build deep learning following on from a teacher's expert introduction.
3. The phrase 'crying intellectually' has been used above to stimulate the reader's thinking. Which teaching techniques do you use to ensure that pupils grapple and persevere with challenging tasks?
4. What examples have you seen in colleagues' classrooms of exciting and innovative approaches to homework which inspire pupils?
5. What particular out-of-class activities (e.g. visitors into class, visits out, forging business and community partners) would you enjoy organising to enhance pupils' learning?
6. Think about a couple of lessons you have taught which have exceeded your expectations in terms of superb response from

pupils. And think of two lessons where you had to work much harder than the pupils, and their responses were limited. Which teaching approaches did you use which proved (a) particularly successful, and (b) less profitable? What were lessons learned for you as a reflective practitioner?

7. What is your preferred format for creating and recording lesson plans? What opportunities do you have to share your plans with colleagues, and look at theirs in order to share best practice?

8. Where do you feel you are making/will be able to make the most significant contribution to your school's curriculum development planning?

EVIDENCE EVIDENCE **EVIDENCE** EVIDENCE **EVIDENCE** EVIDENCE

Demonstrate evidence to your tutor mentor of:

- lesson plans which indicate skilful orchestration of time;

- teaching which demonstrates well-judged interventions which serve to develop pupils' understanding;

- teaching which promotes pupils' love of learning;

- materials and tasks which stimulate intellectual curiosity;

- homework activities which consolidate new learning in a motivating and purposeful way for pupils;

- examples of lesson plans you have amended in the light of teaching experience;

- your contributions to curriculum design and development.

5
Adapt teaching to respond to the strengths and needs of all pupils

5 A teacher must: adapt teaching to respond to the strengths and needs of all pupils

A know when and how to differentiate appropriately, using approaches which enable pupils to be taught effectively

B have a secure understanding of how a range of factors can inhibit pupils' ability to learn, and how best to overcome these

C demonstrate an awareness of the physical, social and intellectual development of children, and know how to adapt teaching to support pupils' education at different stages of development

D have a clear understanding of the needs of all pupils, including those with special educational needs; those of high ability; those with English as an additional language; those with disabilities; and be able to use and evaluate distinctive teaching approaches to engage and support them.

(DfE, 2012a, p8)

COMMENTARY > > > > > > COMMENTARY > > > > > >

One of the striking features of any class of pupils is the sheer diversity and range of interests, aptitudes, aspirations and attitudes towards learning. This is at times memorable, frustrating, enriching, confusing. Standard 5 sets out the clear expectation that teaching needs to be adapted to respond to the strengths and weaknesses of all pupils. This is demanding, whether for the trainee teacher or the experienced practitioner.

The key word 'differentiate' rears its head here, a word readily favoured by classroom observers (whether colleagues, tutors or inspectors) offering feedback on lessons. In fact, the word's regular appearance in the context of feedback highlights just how difficult it can be for even the most skilled teacher to ensure that the needs of *all* pupils are met consistently.

In amplifying the scope of the Standard 5 heading, there are four stated areas for the teacher to focus upon.

A   Whether teaching a so-called mixed ability or setted or banded class, a range of abilities will always exist. Whole-class teaching nearly always has its place, and within that mode of instruction, skilful and open questioning can serve to differentiate effectively. Well judged interventions from the teacher are a hallmark of very good teaching, in any context, from the practical to the more intellectual. The constant challenge for the teacher is knowing when and how to differentiate: at what point in a session to pause to allow independent working; which pupils should work together as a group; which individuals would benefit from focused attention from a learning support assistant; which pupils might gain from following up a question through use of the internet or a self-study programme on the laptop; which pair might go off to the library; how best to deploy (and when) a mini-plenary, led by the teacher or a group of pupils; can homework be usefully differentiated?

B   Knowing pupils' individual learning needs is both explicit and implicit within a number of the Standards. The skilled professional will have a secure knowledge of how different factors can inhibit learning, and what techniques and interventions can be deployed in the best interests of the pupils. Of course, the factors may change in the course of a term or year, and the aware teacher is alert to that change. For some pupils, challenging home circumstances may mean that the school sets aside good facilities for those pupils to do homework. Additional one-to-one reading groups may be needed by other pupils, or catch-up classes in maths. Tracking and evaluating the impact of interventions is essential.

C   Self-evidently, children and young people within the school system develop at different rates and in different ways, physically, socially and intellectually. Skilled early years' practitioners can recognise when young children move from a simple understanding of the concrete to appreciating abstract ideas. Secondary teachers will make perceptive judgements about when to introduce certain challenging and perhaps 'adult' concepts. While working within the programmes outlined in the National Curriculum, school-based curriculum or examination syllabuses, confident teachers make selections about content on a regular basis, tailoring subject matter and new skills to the needs of their pupils.

D   This bullet point builds carefully on the previous three, with a particular focus on four groups of pupils, appreciating always that groups are made up of individuals. There is emphasis too on teachers harnessing distinctive approaches in classrooms, and evaluating their impact, making adjustments as required.

Group 1: teachers in mainstream settings encounter some pupils who find learning in their particular subject really quite difficult: this may be linked to delayed cognitive development, to a pupil's hand-eye coordination, to difficulties with speech or handwriting, to temporary medical problems. The onus is on the teacher (and the school) to have diagnosed the specific learning needs and to have put in place strategies to address them.

Further, it is the responsibility of all teachers to act on an individual pupil's school action plan or statement of special educational needs which might specify different writing equipment, a bespoke space in the classroom with additional lighting, a short note to parents in a pupil's diary at the end of each lesson, or extra time for practical assignments.

Group 2: the education system has often been unhelpful to teachers in the way it has requested schools to identify so-called 'gifted and talented' pupils and to place them on a special register. Schools sometimes miss out on identifying pupils' particular talents. Suffice to say, for the Year 5 teacher who finds two very able mathematicians in her class; for the Year 10 teacher who has two outstanding gymnasts in his GCSE PE class; for the Year 12 teacher who has in her A-level English group, a potential Oxbridge scholar – those pupils' individual needs must be catered for.

Group 3: there are many thousands of pupils in UK schools whose first language is not English (EAL pupils), and whose working knowledge of English varies considerably. Widespread evidence indicates that this fact is rarely an obstacle to good progress and outcomes if teachers are suitably trained in EAL teaching techniques. Recognition of the pupils' heritage language(s) is vital, and for example, dual-language dictionaries may be provided in class. Equally critical is the teacher's avowed ambition to provide scaffolding and support to accelerate pupils' oral and written command of English: the language of school, examinations, university and the workplace ahead.

Group 4: it is important to remember here that disabilities in pupils can be temporary or more permanent, each requiring different, sensitively thought-through approaches. In most schools there are specialists who are able to offer appropriate advice to colleagues, and trainee teachers are strongly advised to avail themselves of this expertise. For teachers in special schools, clearly a complex array of special needs presents itself, requiring tailored interventions rooted in high quality training, and working in a multi-professional classroom.

REFLECTIONS

1. From your own school days, which subject do you remember being particularly good at, or having difficulties with? What interventions and support do you recall as being most effective for you?

2. When first meeting a class, what techniques do you use to gauge pupils' different aptitudes and interests? How do use the school's pupil performance data to help you?

3. When you are giving an introduction to a topic or detailed explanation to a whole-class, how do you check they have understood what you have been saying? Think about your natural style of questioning – is it suitably open?

4. What practice have you observed from other colleagues which enables skilful differentiation within whole-class teaching sessions?

5. What practice have you seen which leads to very good differentiation through individual, paired or small group work? Which teaching and learning techniques have you introduced in your own classroom that have been particularly effective?

6. Reflect on an occasion when you have been successful in adapting your teaching as a response to your keen awareness of a group of pupils' social or intellectual development. What did you do that had a strong impact?

7. For those pupils with a statement of educational needs, which interventions have you seen in colleagues' classrooms that you have judged to be having a significant impact on pupils' progress and outcomes?

8. For high attaining pupils, what materials and interventions have you seen in other classrooms which have impressed you, and which you would like to emulate?

9. What are your own specific training needs to support your teaching of pupils whose first language is not English?

10. Turning back to Standard 1 (page 11), how do you ensure within your classroom teaching, that you set consistently high expectations for pupils with special educational needs?

EVIDENCE EVIDENCE **EVIDENCE** EVIDENCE **EVIDENCE** EVIDENCE

Demonstrate evidence to your tutor mentor of:

- displays which profile the work of pupils of high ability;
- displays which profile the work of pupils with special educational needs or disabilities;
- lesson plans which specify how you are differentiating tasks for high ability pupils;
- classroom and homework materials which are catering for the needs of those pupils with English as an additional language;
- your classroom actions in response to a pupil's statement of special educational needs, including, where appropriate, effective deployment of a learning support assistant;
- questioning techniques which demonstrate skilful differentiation.

6

Make accurate and productive use of assessment

COMMENTARY > > > > > > COMMENTARY > > > > > >

Standard 1 sets down expectations that teachers are accountable for pupils' progress and outcomes. Pivotal to this is a teacher's accurate and productive use of assessment. In common with school systems globally, the explosion of available data and ways of analysing performance within UK schools has given rise to a whole industry of target setting, benchmarking, national and international league tables. This plethora of information can sometimes threaten to overwhelm the teacher. It is important therefore to have a secure grasp of meaningful and relevant data which impacts on your own teaching at classroom level.

In amplifying the scope of the Standard 6 heading, there are four stated areas for teachers to focus upon.

A   Standard 3 outlines the importance of the teacher's good subject and curriculum knowledge. Building on that knowledge in this Standard comes the expectation that a teacher has a secure grasp of how pupils are to be assessed in a given curriculum area: whether as a Reception practitioner involved with the early learning goals; a Year 8 geography teacher ensuring coverage of environmental change and sustainable development; or a Year 11 teacher of design and technology ensuring sufficient time is allocated to students' coursework.

This bullet further highlights the vital importance of teachers knowing well the particular statutory assessment requirements relevant to the age range they are teaching, from phonics tests at age 6 to A2 papers at age 18.

B   The words 'formative' and 'summative' are part of every teacher's armoury of jargon – and it is important to have a clear understanding of the difference between the two. In essence, 'formative' is about informing and shaping the pupil's ongoing work and the teacher's knowledge of those developments; 'summative' comes at the end of a unit, or term, or year, offering a judgement – and usually a grade or mark – on work completed. Formative assessment takes place all the time in class as teachers circulate and correct pupils' work, orally and in writing, and the more experienced the teacher often the more seamless it appears. Summative assessment requires the teacher to know their subject well, and be in a position to apply test or examination criteria to pupils' completed assignments without fear or favour.

C   When well used by teachers, data can have a powerful impact on pupils' progress and overall school improvement. The key for schools and teachers is applying a 'less is more' approach, so that everyone involved has a clear understanding of which data is relevant and which is superfluous. The mark book (whether on paper or online) is every teacher's stock-in-trade, importantly recording pupils' prior attainment data, for example reading ages, cognitive ability test scores, or national curriculum levels attained. The same mark book will include individual targets for pupils which are both challenging and plausible, and which have been agreed as part of a whole-school policy on rigorous target setting.

This evolving data is used not only to record progress and outcomes but, importantly, to inform future lesson planning, including differentiating tasks and assignments to best match pupils' strengths and needs.

D   Feedback is the fuel that propels every pupil's learning. Ask a class of Year 6 or Year 11 pupils what they value about their teacher and prompt, high quality marking will be close to top of the list. 'Marking' in music, physical education, design and technology, history or English comes in different forms, but at the heart of effective classrooms is the teacher's determination to comment on strengths and identify next steps in the best interests of the pupil. Oral feedback can be just as valuable as written. A key adjective in this bullet point is 'regular' – marking needs to be prompt, regular and focused, and is usually shaped by whole-school or departmental guidance.

Finally: teachers spend a lot of time marking and making comments in exercise books and folders. Ask yourself the question: do I give enough time to the pupils to read what I have written? The answer is too often 'no'. Pupils need to have time set aside to respond to the teacher's feedback – that way progress lies.

REFLECTIONS

1. What national and international benchmarking of pupils and schools systems do you know about? How does your school harness this benchmarking?

2. How are pupils in your school performing in the core subjects of English and mathematics relative to local and national statistics?

3. Reflect on how performance data is used in your school. Do you have a secure grasp of the data which is relevant to your classroom? Do you have any training needs, for example with understanding Raiseonline (the Ofsted/DfE interactive system, Reporting and Analysis for Improvement through School Self-Evaluation)?

4. What background reading have you done to ensure you have a good command of statutory assessments relevant to the pupils you are teaching? What in-service training have you had to help you with summative assessment?

5. Observing in other classrooms, what practice have you seen in 'formative' assessment which has impressed you? How does the skilled teacher embed the process of formative assessment in classroom practice?

6. Which habits are you establishing in accurate record-keeping of pupils' performance data? Is your mark book set out in such a way that, if you were absent for a week, a colleague could understand its contents? Or your line manager could use it to gain a quick overview of pupils' progress in your class?

7. What kind of target setting have you done which pupils find useful and motivating? What best practice have you seen in colleagues' classrooms?

8. What examples of 'next-best-step' marking have you been shown or seen through observations?

9. Reflect on your emerging management of marking books and folders promptly and regularly. What habits of good time management are you establishing?

EVIDENCE EVIDENCE **EVIDENCE** EVIDENCE **EVIDENCE** EVIDENCE

Demonstrate evidence to your tutor mentor of:

* your knowledge of your school's overall performance data;

* your knowledge of data relevant to the pupils you are teaching;

* a mark-book (or similar) which has detailed and accurate records of pupils' progress and performance;

* lesson plans which have been adapted and differentiated in the light of assessments you have made of pupils' work;

* good quality 'next-best-step' marking;

* in your classroom practice, good examples of formative assessment, oral and in writing.

Interlude: visiting a Year 6 classroom

(a) When you visit a colleague's upper primary classroom, use the following as a checklist against which you observe.

(b) At the end of a given week, use the questions to help you reflect on your own best practice, and where you might wish to fine-tune your own classroom.

(c) Add your own questions to the checklist, as you develop your skills and experiences.

Questions to ask

1. What are your first impressions of the learning environment?

   - *Is it light, airy and the right temperature for learning?*
   - *Does the classroom, and the areas around it, reflect the range of Y6/ upper primary work? What is special, or striking, about this work?*
   - *Is the classroom arranged so that all children can be involved in discussions and also use their workspace to write, design and implement?*
   - *How do the children react to your presence as a visitor? To what extent are they happy to talk and explain?*
   - *Is it clear that the Y6 class is not merely involved in a SATs revision exercise – or, if this is the case, how is this being managed to maximise learning?*

2. In what ways does the style of teaching and learning reflect that this is a Year 6 class and therefore distinctive in terms of the completion of the primary stage of learning?

3. How is the furniture configured? Are children sitting on the carpet for too long? Where does the teacher position her/himself?

4. To what extent do the children take control of their learning and how able are they to explore a range of learning areas? Are the children aware of what will come next in terms of their move to the secondary stage?

5. In the time you are in the room, count the minutes (a) the teacher talks, and (b) children converse with a proper focus. Is the teacher working harder than the students? Are the children responding easily and readily to the task/stimuli provided?

6. How are support staff being deployed, to have a significant impact on learning?

7. What evidence can you see of Year 6's independent learning skills? If the teacher left the room, would the children continue to work on the current task?

8. Is the level of work appropriate for the more able learners and is it sufficiently demanding? Has the work been effectively scaffolded, while retaining an intrinsic interest/challenge, for those who have learning or personal management difficulties?

9. Is homework or other independent study/research important to the lesson being observed? Has there been some form of lead-in and are there possibilities for extension?

10. How creatively are book/technology resources harnessed to stimulate students' interest and extend their skills and knowledge?

11. Can you tell from looking at books/folders whether the children fully understand what is expected from this lesson/topic ('the story of their learning')? Is there a difference in the way that girls and boys approach this lesson?

12. Are targets for individuals and groups in place? Do the children clearly understand what is expected of them? Is the marking formative and helpful to the child so that s/he can progress?

7

Manage behaviour effectively to ensure a good and safe learning environment

7 A teacher must: manage behaviour effectively to ensure a good and safe learning environment

A have clear rules and routines for behaviour in classrooms, and take responsibility for promoting good and courteous behaviour both in classrooms and around the school, in accordance with the school's behaviour policy

B have high expectations of behaviour, and establish a framework for discipline with a range of strategies, using praise, sanctions and rewards consistently and fairly

C manage classes effectively, using approaches which are appropriate to pupils' needs in order to involve and motivate them

D maintain good relationships with pupils, exercise appropriate authority, and act decisively when necessary.

(DfE, 2012a, p8)

COMMENTARY > > > > > > COMMENTARY > > > > > >

All around the world parents send their children to school each day. Ask any parent what they expect of a school and the most likely reply will come that they expect their child to be safe, happy and well looked after. Learning will follow. It is important for teachers to remember that they are *in loco parentis* at all times, and thus have a core responsibility for ensuring a good and safe learning environment. For some pupils, schools provide a stability and welcoming environment that they may not always experience at home.

When pupils feel secure in their school environment, their self-esteem and motivation are lifted, and they are more likely to be ready for positive learning and engagement with their teachers. This is as true of a young child in Year 1 as it is of a sixth-former in his last year of college.

In amplifying the scope of the Standard 7 heading, there are four stated areas for teachers to focus upon.

A   There are a number of aspects here which are built on in the subsequent bullet points. One clear expectation comes in the phrase 'in accordance with the school's behaviour policy', a reminder that teachers need to act consistently within an overall school framework if behaviour is to be well managed. Remember: pupils thrive on a consistency of approach, and are quick to exploit inconsistencies. Rules and routines are often set down at a whole-school level and it is important that they are followed through by individual teachers. In good schools, pupils and staff treat each other with dignity, courteously, whether in classrooms, corridors or playgrounds. Every teacher has his or her part to play.

B   In the same way that Standard 1 talks of high expectations which motivate pupils, teachers need to demonstrate at all times that they have high expectations of pupils' behaviours and attitudes to learning. Pupils very often have a strong sense of right and wrong – and are quick to express their feelings on the subject – so it is vital that sanctions and rewards are applied consistently and fairly. Trainee teachers might well be given a mentor on the staff to help them with this. There is another word here which requires thoughtful interpretation: 'praise'. It is important that when praise is given, it is earned, and not given for something trivial or which other pupils perceive as undeserved. This is not an easy balance to get right every day, but it is critical to do so to ensure a positive discipline framework.

C   Within a consistent and well applied discipline framework, teachers manage classes in many different ways, and rightly so as this aspect of teaching is closely linked to a teacher's individual personality. What might work for one teacher may not for another, although it is always instructive to observe how skilful staff manage challenging pupils. Whatever strategies are employed, the focus is on involving and motivating pupils to learn and gain maximum benefit from the lessons.

Amongst many features that might be listed, the following are worth noting when observing others and reflecting on one's own practice: the teacher's body language and voice projection; the teacher's position and movement around the classroom; room temperature and light; the teacher's knowledge of every pupil's name; rules around talking and listening; managing transitions; accessibility to pupils of resources; the appearance of the teacher's own desk and the storage of pupils' books; furniture configuration; designated seating plans. Most schools have a checklist of helpful, school-specific tips to support new teachers.

D   Good teaching is built upon teachers establishing a professional and personal rapport with those they teach. This varies depending on the age of the pupils but lies at the core of a successful classroom. There is no substitute for humour, warmth and well-judged challenge and support, delivered in a tone of voice that at once shows the pupils that the teacher cares and is being fair in their dealings. Even the youngest pupils are quick to recognise the teacher who talks down to them, while teenagers can be rightly riled by indiscriminate sarcasm from teachers.

Further, this bullet is worded carefully in expecting teachers to 'exercise appropriate authority' and 'act decisively'. Individual schools will give guidance on this, highlighting the need to act professionally and promptly, where the occasion arises.

REFLECTIONS

1. What is your understanding of the phrase *in loco parentis* as it applies in your school context?
2. What evidence have you seen of pupils reacting well to a good, welcoming environment, and reacting negatively to a poor environment?
3. Reading through your school's behaviour policy, what seem to be its strengths, and perhaps weaknesses? Which aspects of the policy seem to be most effective with pupils? Are pupils involved in keeping the policy under review?
4. What have you learned from observing colleagues about how (a) sanctions and (b) praise are used to positive effect?
5. Reflect on the list of features in bullet C above – what techniques are you developing to ensure good classroom management?

6. Think of examples in your school setting (and on school visits) where you have been or might be called upon to 'act decisively' and 'exercise appropriate authority'.

7. The following is taken from the Ofsted school inspection handbook. It describes what the features are of a school where behaviour is outstanding. What do you think of these descriptors? Would you amend or add anything?

Outstanding (1)

- Pupils' attitudes to learning are exemplary.
- Parents, staff and pupils are unreservedly positive about both behaviour and safety.
- Pupils' behaviour outside lessons is almost always impeccable. Pupils' pride in the school is shown by their excellent conduct, manners and punctuality.
- Pupils are fully aware of different forms of bullying, including cyber-bullying and prejudice-based bullying, and actively try to prevent it from occurring. Bullying in all its forms is rare and dealt with highly effectively.
- Skilled and highly consistent behaviour management by all staff makes a strong contribution to an exceptionally positive climate for learning. There are excellent improvements in behaviour over time for individuals or groups with particular behaviour needs.

(Ofsted, 2012a, p40)

EVIDENCE EVIDENCE **EVIDENCE** EVIDENCE **EVIDENCE** EVIDENCE

Demonstrate evidence to your tutor mentor of:

- a welcoming physical environment which has a positive effect on pupils' well-being;
- display of rules and/or routines which you expect from pupils;
- your good working knowledge of the school's behaviour policy;
- you demonstrating the effective use of praise with pupils;
- your effective use of (one of) the school's sanctions;
- examples of where you have had an impact on behaviour beyond your own classroom, for example with pupils at breaktimes.

8
Fulfil wider professional responsibilities

8 A teacher must: fulfil wider professional responsibilities

A make a positive contribution to the wider life and ethos of the school

B develop effective professional relationships with colleagues, knowing how and when to draw on advice and specialist support

C deploy support staff effectively

D take responsibility for improving teaching through appropriate professional development, responding to advice and feedback from colleagues

E communicate effectively with parents with regard to pupils' achievements and well-being.

(DfE, 2012a, p9)

COMMENTARY > > > > > > COMMENTARY > > > > > >

A well-respected book about schooling, published in the 1970s, was titled *Fifteen Thousand Hours* (Rutter et al., 1979). This was approximately the amount of time that the average child between ages 5 and 16 spent in school. A quick bit of maths suggests this hasn't changed much over the decades! Most of those hours are spent by pupils in classrooms, for which teachers have a lead responsibility. This Standard reminds teachers that their professional role is not confined to the classroom but extends more widely. Many experienced practitioners would at once say that there is as much enjoyment and fulfilment to be had in the wider school context as there is amidst the buzz of the classroom.

Standard 8 usefully rounds off Part 1 of the Teachers' Standards, in some ways both echoing the Preamble and serving as a preface to Part 2: Personal and Professional Conduct.

In amplifying the scope of the Standard 8 heading, there are five stated areas for teachers to focus upon.

A   Schools are busy, diverse and interesting places to work, whether a small rural primary school or a large urban secondary comprehensive. Each has its own character and personalities, its ways of doing, history, traditions, quirks and future planning. It is not difficult therefore to find real fulfilment in contributing to the wider life of the school and shaping its ethos. Volunteering to accompany pupils on school journeys, taking sports teams, running a drama or IT or library club, leading maths or literacy booster sessions, taking assemblies, leading staff training – there are many ways in which teachers new to the profession can make a difference to pupils outside classrooms. At the same time you are signalling to the headteacher your professional ambitions to be seen as more than a classroom teacher.

Remember: the whole-school community benefits when you share your particular skills and interests.

B   At times, teaching can feel a solitary activity, the teacher on their own with a class of pupils. But this is rare. Good schools' strengths lie in their collegiality, with teaching, support and administrative staff (and governors) always prepared to work together in the best interests of the pupils and fellow staff members. It is important to work hard at establishing positive relationships with close colleagues, drawing on the support of line managers and others with particular expertise, for example special educational needs colleagues, speech therapists, learning mentors. Trainee teachers will have a school-based tutor, and it is reasonable to look to this person to help you sort any teething problems you encounter in your first few months in a school.

A confident leadership team will also take advantage of your 'fresh eyes', and while the eyes are still fresh ask you if you can suggest any ways in which the school might improve its routines and systems.

C   Depending on your school setting and the age range you teach, you may well have regular support in your classroom from teaching/learning assistants. It is a feature of best early years' practice that teachers, support staff and nursery nurses plan learning activities together; at times in those classrooms it is difficult for a casual observer to say who is the teacher and who is the support member. Through primary school, most class teachers will have some kind of other adult presence, and it is the teacher's key responsibility to ensure that additional support is effectively deployed. This may be designated work with a child with special educational needs; or it may be leading a guided reading group or a maths extension session; and this may take place within the classroom or in a neighbouring space. The teacher retains overall responsibility for the quality of the intervention work and for monitoring pupils' progress.

In a secondary context, teachers may also expect to have in their class-rooms colleagues supporting pupils with special educational needs, or it can be that the class has a learning/behaviour mentor accompanying designated pupils. For subject specialists in a number of practical subjects, technicians often work alongside pupils – here again, it is the teacher's role to ensure that deployment is well planned and purposeful. Remember: it is important that support staff are well led by classroom teachers in order that their impact on pupils is significant and good value for money is demonstrated.

D   This bullet opens with a trenchant phrase: 'take responsibility for'. For the new entrant to the profession, there is a particular imperative to learn quickly, whether in relation to developing knowledge of statutory assess-ment or in building classroom management skills. In a school you soon learn who are the 'go-to' teachers, those whom you can readily approach for advice and encouragement. It is important to seek out feedback, formal and informal, to try out new ways of doing, and to respond to advice as appropriate. To echo a point above: it is trust and mutual respect which leads to genuine collegiality, in any work setting. You learn quickly, and perhaps by trial and error, whose fine judgement you can trust and whose good practice you hope will shape your own.

Schools are places of learning, not only for the pupils but also for the staff. It is vital that teachers avail themselves of purposeful continuous profes-sional development. This can be school-based, led by teachers who are expert in, say, working with higher attaining pupils or managing group work in classrooms. And trainee teachers will usually have some kind of induc-tion programme in their first year, covering a range of relevant topics. Equally, courses, conferences and study opportunities beyond the school can provide an invaluable way to stay fresh and keep up-to-date as a teacher. (Chapter 13 offers a list of titles to extend your horizons!)

E   Many schools in their prospectuses make explicit the pivotal triangle of communication and relationships between teachers, pupils and parents. That three-way partnership is vital to a school's overall well-being. The school has a core responsibility to communicate effectively with parents: to communicate regularly and in a way that is accessible to all parents. In working with parents, teachers usually operate within an overall framework or protocol set down by the school to prevent misunderstandings and unrealistic expectations. And of course the primary setting, within which parents meet each other at the school gate and are often in classrooms as volunteers, is a different beast from the inevitably more distant secondary school where alternative ways of working with parents need to operate.

Whatever systems and timetables are in place, and consistent with school policy and practice, it is a teacher's responsibility to ensure that parents are kept well informed of their children's achievements and well-being, through regular and clear communication.

REFLECTIONS

1. What has drawn you into the teaching profession? Are you as excited by what you can contribute to the school as a whole as by the buzz of the classroom?

2. What particular skills, expertise and interests will you take to any school you work in?

3. Which staff with specialist knowledge have you gone to for advice? Were you able to act on that advice?

4. As a 'fresh pair of eyes' on your school, what thoughts are you presenting to the leadership team about what works well and what could be improved in the school?

5. What good examples have you observed of support staff in class-rooms being well deployed and having a strong learning impact on pupils?

6. How have you harnessed effectively any support staff you have worked with? What planning documents and materials did you provide for them? What expectations did you set out to ensure high impact on pupils' learning?

7. What is the quality of the induction programme in your school? What are its strengths, and how are you helping to shape and improve its contents? What wider reading or great websites for classroom use have you suggested to colleagues?

8. What are the characteristics of the 'go-to' teachers in your school?

9. Do you have a clear understanding of the school's expectations of how you should communicate with parents? What training needs do you have in this area?

EVIDENCE EVIDENCE **EVIDENCE** EVIDENCE **EVIDENCE** EVIDENCE

Demonstrate evidence to your tutor mentor of:

- your knowledge of the wider life of the school you are teaching in: e.g. its traditions, extra-curricular strengths, governors' involvement, ethos, etc.;

- advice and feedback you have received which has helped improve your classroom practice;

- lesson plans which demonstrate your skilful deploying of teaching assistants or other adults;

- contributions you have made to school-based in-service training;

- current wider reading and (perhaps) action research which is informing your practice;

- successes you have enjoyed in communicating with parents.

9
Personal and professional conduct

COMMENTARY > > > > > > COMMENTARY > > > > > >

By way of background: in the accompanying DfE notes on the Teachers' Standards 2012, it makes clear that Part 2 of the document replaces the

General Teaching Council for England's *Code of Conduct and Practice for Registered Teachers*, which ceased to have effect on September 1st, 2012.

The DfE notes also make clear that in order to meet the Standards, a trainee or teacher will need to demonstrate that 'their practice is consistent with the definition set out in the Preamble, and that they have met the standards in both Part 1 and Part 2' (DfE, 2012a, para 12, p4).

The Preamble and Part 2 should be read together. They provide a bedrock for the profession. Teachers should scrutinise carefully what is being expected of them, whether in their first or thirtieth year of teaching, and reflect thoughtfully on the carefully chosen words and phrases set out above.

REFLECTIONS

1. 'At all times observing proper boundaries appropriate to a teacher's professional position.'
   What does that mean in practice for you, as a new entrant into the profession? Think ahead. What situations might arise where you have to make prompt judgements about what to do or not do, in order to observe proper boundaries?

2. What does the term 'safeguarding' mean to you? Do you have a secure working understanding of the school's safeguarding procedures, and your responsibilities within them? Rehearse your understanding with an experienced colleague.

3. In what kind of situations might you find yourself having to balance the rights of different pupils? Think about some possible scenarios and your proposed actions. Again, talk these through with another colleague who has a very good knowledge of the pupils and families at your school.

4. 'Not undermining fundamental British values, etc.'
   The DfE notes indicate that the phrase 'fundamental British values is taken from the definition of extremism as articulated in the Prevent Strategy, launched in June 2011' (DfE 2012a, p5). Discuss with a couple of colleagues how this aspect of expected conduct might arise in your school.

5. Do you have any strongly held beliefs, for example with regard to politics, religion or social mores? How do you make sure that in the classroom these beliefs do not 'exploit pupils' vulnerability'?

6. Teachers must act within statutory frameworks. The DfE notes state: 'Statutory frameworks includes all legal requirements... The term also covers the professional duties of teachers as set out in the statutory School Teachers' Pay and Conditions Document.' Familiarise yourself with the most recent Pay and Conditions document to see how what is set out there complements the Teachers' Standards (DfE 2012b).

    Looking back through Part 2 of the Teachers' Standards, what aspects of conduct do you think are going to provide you with the greatest challenges in your early months and years of teaching?

Interlude: visiting a Year 10 classroom

Read through the following questions which aim to help you reflect on and analyse best practice.

(a) When you visit a colleague's upper secondary classroom, use the following as a checklist against which you observe.

(b) At the end of a given week, use the questions to help you reflect on your own best practice, and where you might wish to fine-tune your own classroom.

(c) Add your own questions to the checklist as you develop your own skills in lesson observations.

Questions to ask

1. What are your first impressions of the learning environment?

   - *is it light, airy and the right temperature for learning?*
   - *does the room celebrate the specialist subject being taught?*
   - *does the room celebrate Year 10 work?*
   - *how do the students react to your presence as a visitor?*

2. In what ways does the style of teaching and learning reflect that this is a Year 10 class and not a Year 7 class? (e.g. How is furniture configured? Where does the teacher position her/himself?)

3. In the time you are in the room, count the minutes (a) the teacher talks, and (b) students converse with a proper focus. Is the teacher working harder than the students?

4. What evidence can you see of Year 10's independent learning skills? If the teacher left the room, would students' focus continue?

5. Are the students teaching?

6. Is the level of work appropriate for more able students, irrespective of mixed-ability or setted group? If not, how would you make it more demanding?

7. How has homework led into this lesson? How is homework/further independent study/research following up the lesson?

8. What evidence is there of (a) fun, (b) scholarship, (c) intriguing digressions, or (d) the teacher sharing personal enthusiasms?

9. How well does the teacher demonstrate his/her own specialist subject knowledge? Does s/he extend horizons and leave students magically wondering?

10. How creatively are book/technology resources harnessed to stimulate students' interest and extend their skills and knowledge?

11. Can you tell from looking at books/folders whether students fully understand syllabus demands ('the story of their learning')? Is there a difference in the quality of note-taking and storage, between girls and boys?

12. Are targets for individuals and groups in place? Is marking formative and advising how a student can improve from say, GCSE grade B to grade A? Do students know what A* quality in the subject looks like?

13. How is the teaching *deepening* pupils' knowledge and skills?

10
Master Teacher

The Teachers' Standards 2012 came into being as the first part of a Review established by the Secretary of State for Education in 2011. The second part of the Review led to recommendations that a Master Teacher (MT) Standard also be established. At the time of publication of this book, such a Standard is still under consideration.

For those teachers who see themselves developing strongly within the profession, what is set out below is worth reading and reflecting on, whether or not the MT Standard is taken up in some way formally by government and the profession.

The MT Standard is rooted in international best practice and what some of the world's most successful school systems expect of their teachers. It presents a focused definition of those teachers who are demonstrating excellent practice, and, in the words of the Review, 'who have the potential to make the most significant and positive impact on their pupils, their peers and on the profession as a whole' (DfE, 2011b, p3).

Further, the Standard shows how an excellent teacher, working across the full breadth of the Teachers' Standards, might demonstrate consistently the very best of classroom practice.

For trainee teachers, the Master Teacher narrative descriptions (each of just three paragraphs) might stand as aspirational, a goal ahead to be achieved following a few years of demonstrating consistently excellent practice and making a decisive impact over time on their pupils. For all reflective practitioners, the descriptions could be seen as 'extension expectations' when compared with the main Teachers' Standards.

The MT Standard begins with an introduction, an echo of the Preamble to the main Teachers' Standards. It is followed by five sections which in many ways usefully distil the essence of what it is to be a highly skilled classroom practitioner. The five domains – knowledge, classroom performance, outcomes, environment and ethos, professional context – are commonly to be found in the professional expectations of teachers across the world, from Finland to Singapore, USA to New Zealand, Dubai to Germany.

Following the Master Teacher Standard text below, there is a series of Reflections to help you interrogate the text.

THE MASTER TEACHER STANDARD

This Standard should be read as part of a profile of a Master Teacher who may have his or her own particular strengths in specific areas. Above all, a Master Teacher is someone whose professionalism has come to be seen as an integral part of his or her character.

Master Teachers are excellent teachers, deeply committed to making a difference to the lives of their pupils. The Master Teacher is a self-assured presence in the classroom, who effortlessly captures pupils' imagination.

Although Master Teachers may take on management and other roles in the school, there is no presumption that they will move outside the classroom. They are exceptional practitioners, for whom high levels of performance in the basic Teachers' Standards are taken as given. They are enthusiastic about their specialism or subject(s) (see Note 1 below). They have a strong sense of the significance of what they teach in the context of the whole curriculum and beyond.

A. Knowledge

Master Teachers have deep and extensive knowledge of their specialism, going far beyond the set programmes they teach. They have an intrinsic curiosity about their specialism, keep up with developments, and their teaching reflects their own passion and expertise. They respond intelligently and confidently to the unexpected and wide-ranging questions their pupils are encouraged to ask, and they are able to lead discussions and explorations which take pupils beyond the confines of teaching programmes.

They are able to teach their specialism clearly, intelligently and inventively, showing considerable breadth and initiative. They have a keen sense of the most effective and engaging ways of communicating the subject matter to pupils of all abilities and aptitudes.

Master Teachers are reflective and self-critical regarding their own teaching and make critical appraisals of new developments and techniques, which they use judiciously. A thorough understanding of the developmental and social backgrounds of pupils further supports and informs their practice.

B. Classroom Performance

Master Teachers command the classroom, skilfully leading, encouraging and extending pupils (see Note 2 below). They have the respect of both pupils and parents. They are at ease in their role, and discipline and dialogue are unselfconscious and effective.

Teaching is motivating, often inspiring, and basic principles are expertly taught. Expectations are challengingly high, realistic, based on sound experience, and take into account the abilities of all pupils. The pacing of lessons is well orchestrated and transitions between whole class teaching, group and individual work are seamless. Questioning and discussion are of a high order, relevant and at times deep.

Pupils are consistently focused and engaged in their studies, and are encouraged effectively to reflect on their own progress. Homework and independent study activities are wisely chosen to extend the range and depth of pupils' knowledge, understanding and acquisition of skills. Master Teachers ensure that high quality assessment and feedback are consistently prompt, rigorous and constructive. They enable pupils to identify and remedy their misunderstandings and build on their successes. They promote pupils' desire to seek and apply their knowledge further.

C. Outcomes

The Master Teacher's meticulous planning and organisation ensure that pupils are well-prepared for all forms of assessment. Outcomes achieved by pupils in the context in question are outstanding. They have an awareness of school, national and international benchmarks and examination reports, including data from maintained and independent schools.

Master Teachers have an extensive understanding of and expertise in relevant assessment systems and examinations. They make critical use of data, relating to the prior and current performance of pupils, to underpin and motivate improvement. As a result, pupils understand what they are learning and have a strong grasp of the principles on which the knowledge and capacities in question are based.

Outcomes are also outstanding in a more informal sense. Pupils not only understand what they have been taught and its significance, and are able to deploy this knowledge critically and analytically, but they are inspired to go beyond what they have been taught.

D. Environment and Ethos

The class is one in which pupils feel welcome and valued. There is a stimulating culture of scholarship alongside a sense of mutual respect and good manners. The Master Teacher has an excellent rapport with classes and with individual pupils.

The classroom environment created to support study and activities is an inspirational example of practice, appropriate to the age range or phase. Resources, including books and IT, are well-chosen and stimulating, contributing significantly to progress in lessons. Resources excite, extend and support different abilities, interests and aptitudes.

In classrooms for younger pupils, visual stimuli arising from children's own work offer powerful models to which other children can aspire. In classrooms for older pupils, scholarship is also evident in the classroom surroundings. Displays often reflect contemporary events and a breadth of subject matter which extend beyond the subject under study.

E. Professional Context

Master Teachers are highly regarded by colleagues, who want to learn from them. They willingly play a role in the development of school policies and in the professional life of the school. They work in collaboration with colleagues on pastoral and wider pupil-related matters, giving advice as appropriate. They engage with and contribute to professional networks beyond the school.

They are analytical in evaluating and developing their own craft and knowledge, making full use of continuing professional development and appropriate research. They recognise the vital importance of out-of-school and extra-curricular activities, both academically and personally, and play a leading role here and in the wider life of the school.

Master Teachers are open in the giving and receiving of professional advice, which may include coaching or mentoring colleagues and less-experienced teachers. They work to significant effect with other adults in ensuring high quality education for the pupils they serve.

(Notes:

1. References to 'specialism' should be taken to mean 'subject(s) or specialisms'.
2. 'Classroom' should be read as extending to all other environments in which Master Teachers work.)

(DfE, 2011b, pp9–11)

REFLECTIONS

1. What are your thoughts on the idea of a Master Teacher Standard? Is it useful for the profession to have a narrative describing excellent practice?
2. Do you think the Introduction to the MT Standard (page 58) builds constructively on the Preamble to the main Teachers' Standards?

Would you wish to see anything else added, from your own experiences?

3. What do you think of the descriptions in the 'Knowledge' section? In what ways is this a more demanding set of expectations than is to be found in Teachers' Standard 3?

4. In the 'Classroom Performance' section, the bar is set high: 'command' in the classroom; 'inspiring' teaching; expectations 'challengingly high'; and assessment and feedback are 'consistently prompt, rigorous and constructive'. What examples have you seen in classrooms of some or all of the points listed? Where do your emerging strengths lie?

5. While Teachers' Standard 2 is headed progress and outcomes, the MT Standard simply states 'Outcomes', a reflection of international best practice. Is it important to make the notion of 'progress' explicit or not? Why, or why not?

6. The MT Standard is short and pithy, by its nature and design. Try drafting a fourth paragraph to add to the 'Environment and Ethos' section, directly linked to the age range you are teaching.

7. How important in your view is the final section 'Professional Context'? Is it your experience to date that teachers generally see themselves occupying this wider, outward-facing professional role?

8. In observing experienced colleagues, what else do they do which you find highly effective with pupils and professionally exciting, and which might be added to a revised set of Master Teacher Standards?

11
Ofsted's Evaluation of the Quality of Teaching

Ofsted School Inspection Handbook: Evaluating the Quality of Teaching

Grade descriptors – Quality of teaching in the school

(Note: These descriptors should not be used as a checklist. They must be applied adopting a 'best fit' approach which relies on the professional judgement of the inspection team. The grade descriptors describe the quality of teaching in the school as a whole, taking account of evidence over time. While they include some characteristics of individual lessons, they are not designed to be used to judge individual lessons.)

Outstanding (1)

- Much of the teaching in all key stages and most subjects is outstanding and never less than consistently good. As a result, almost all pupils currently on roll in the school, including disabled pupils, those who have special educational needs and those for whom the pupil premium provides support, are making rapid and sustained progress.
- All teachers have consistently high expectations of all pupils. They plan and teach lessons that enable pupils to learn exceptionally well across the curriculum.
- Teachers systematically and effectively check pupils' understanding throughout lessons, anticipating where they may need to intervene and doing so with notable impact on the quality of learning.
- The teaching of reading, writing, communication and mathematics is highly effective and cohesively planned and implemented across the curriculum.
- Teachers and other adults generate high levels of engagement and commitment to learning across the whole school.
- Consistently high quality marking and constructive feedback from teachers ensure that pupils make rapid gains.

- Teachers use well-judged and often inspirational teaching strategies, including setting appropriate homework that, together with sharply focused and timely support and intervention, match individual needs accurately. Consequently, pupils learn exceptionally well across the curriculum.

Good (2)

- Teaching in most subjects, including English and mathematics, is usually good, with examples of some outstanding teaching. As a result, most pupils and groups of pupils currently on roll in the school, including disabled pupils, those who have special educational needs, and those for whom the pupil premium provides support, make good progress and achieve well over time.
- Teachers have high expectations. They plan and teach lessons that deepen pupils' knowledge and understanding and enable them to develop a range of skills across the curriculum.
- Teachers listen to, carefully observe and skilfully question pupils during lessons in order to reshape tasks and explanations to improve learning.
- Reading, writing, communication and mathematics are taught effectively.
- Teachers and other adults create a positive climate for learning in their lessons and pupils are interested and engaged.
- Teachers assess pupils' learning and progress regularly and accurately. They ensure that pupils know how well they have done and what they need to do to improve.
- Effective teaching strategies, including setting appropriate homework, and appropriately targeted support and intervention are matched well to most pupils' individual needs, including those most and least able, so that pupils learn well in lessons.

Requires improvement (3)

- Teaching requires improvement as it is not good.

Inadequate (4)

Teaching is likely to be inadequate where any of the following apply:

- As a result of weak teaching over time, pupils or particular groups of pupils including disabled pupils, those who have special educational needs, and those for whom the pupil premium provides support, are making inadequate progress.
- Pupils cannot communicate, read, write, or apply mathematics as well as they should.
- Teachers do not have sufficiently high expectations and teaching over time fails to engage or interest particular groups of pupils, including disabled pupils and those who have special educational needs.
- Learning activities are not sufficiently well matched to the needs of pupils.

(Ofsted, 2012a, pp36–7)

COMMENTARY > > > > > > COMMENTARY > > > > > >

Teachers across England are familiar with the work of Ofsted and its school inspectors. Since its creation in 1992, Ofsted has operated various inspection frameworks. From September 2012, schools are being judged under five principal headings:

- Overall effectiveness
- Achievement of pupils
- Quality of teaching
- Behaviour and safety
- Leadership and management

The significant change in this framework from previous versions is that while previously Grade 3 indicated 'satisfactory', Grade 3 now indicates 'requires improvement'. This is a clear statement to all teachers and all schools that pupils everywhere deserve at least good or better practices, provision and outcomes. (See Roy Blatchford's article on page 77.)

The Teachers' Standards 2012 set out expectations which are intended to lead to good practice being the norm across the country. As you read over the Standards and compare what Ofsted outlines above in relation to teaching, you should come across much common ground. Of course, teachers should have a secure understanding of the whole inspection framework, not just that relating to teaching.

A further note: Teachers' Standard 1 reads:

Set high expectations which inspire, motivate and challenge pupils

Ofsted's definition of good teaching has, as bullet point two:

Teachers have high expectations

There is a coming together in the two documents which spells out roundly just how important it is that teachers everywhere pitch their expectations in a way that will genuinely get the best from every individual pupil, no matter which classroom she or he is in.

REFLECTIONS

1. Looking at the four bullet points which Ofsted indicates are characteristic of inadequate teaching, which of the Teachers' Standards focuses on each of these points? Make a short set of notes, related to your own classroom, which will serve as a strong aide-memoire as to how to avoid any inadequacies, as described by Ofsted.

2. Reread the Note relating to the grade descriptors (page 63). Why is this important for teachers, schools and inspectors?

3. Run through Ofsted's definitions of good teaching. Match up each of the bullet points with a corresponding statement in the Teachers' Standards. Are there any aspects which don't readily correspond?

4. School inspection frameworks in different parts of the world rely on a stock of comparative adjectives and adverbs to indicate different levels of competency and progression. If you look at the Ofsted example above, it is no exception. Pick out (a) the adjectives, and (b) the adverbs that signal the difference between good and outstanding practice.

5. In your own classroom, how can you secure consistently 'good' practice? Which aspects need particular focus?

6. Which aspects of your practice do you think can soon touch 'outstanding'? In what respects (look at the adjectives and adverbs again) do you think the bar is set very high for Grade 1, and will require concerted efforts to achieve?

7. Seek out opportunities to do some lesson co-observations with an experienced colleague, using both the Ofsted framework and the Teachers' Standards. Use the notes which you write to (a) offer constructive feedback to colleagues, and (b) reflect on your own practices.

12
Successful schools, successful teachers

So what is the cocktail of very good schools where teachers want to be, and which enjoy parental and student confidence, in the UK and globally?

All around the school there are places of interest, challenge, wonder and reflection. The student voice is listened to and acted upon. The staff is committed to excellent teaching and an orderly, enthusiastic community. The leadership of the school promotes an aspirational culture – one of belief that children and young people can achieve more than they might have thought. Governors, parents and local people hold the school in high regard, and are involved in productive discourse about its vision and performance.

In summary, certain aspects stand out from the norm, both to those who work in the school, and to visitors who observe: 'Someone's doing something special here'.

And it's all about execution. It is not enough to get the ideas right; they have to be adopted. It is not enough to adopt them; they have to be implemented correctly. And it is not enough to implement them correctly; they have to be constantly reviewed and adjusted over time as leaders see what works and what doesn't. Steve Jobs proclaimed a similar mantra at Apple, encouraging his workforce to 'fail wisely' in developing new products.

We are all deeply interested in doing better tomorrow what we did today. All the most successful schools I know are restless to get better. They simply aren't content to stand still. So what do they do?

Five steps

First, they interrogate current routines; they confront comfortable orthodoxies; they challenge why they do what they do, from minor practical details to major policies.

Second, they harness a wide range of carefully gathered data, qualitative and quantitative; they know what pupils, staff, parents, governors, the wider community identify as strengths and relative weaknesses.

Third, they respond with timely, small-scale innovation pinpointed on a clear aspect for development. Committed 'can do' innovators on the staff show that a hitherto intractable problem can be solved, thoughtfully, and at the right pace for the school community.

Fourth, the small-scale innovation wins the hearts and minds of others. Gradually, whole-scale innovation takes root. Experiences and outcomes for pupils and staff are enriched.

Fifth – and to complete the virtuous circle – the school has now moved to a higher operational level; it is in a position to interrogate its routines from a better place.

Restless schools are the ones that flourish. Reviewing and adjusting over time is the key to reinvigorating any business. Otherwise, stagnation beckons.

Good to Outstanding

Digging beneath the surface of the restless school questing for excellence, unsurprisingly you will find that there is a lot going on, though the staff may not be shouting about it – they are happily focused. What are these key features within the UK system, shaped significantly by the Ofsted inspection framework?

When schools receive a 'good' Ofsted inspection, they decide that to achieve 'outstanding' is a natural next step. Senior leaders ask all staff to read the reports of schools which have been judged 'outstanding'. Staff then commit themselves to ensuring that the same kind of phrases they have been reading in 'outstanding' reports can, in time, be readily written about their own school. Schools place great emphasis on everyone in the school knowing and understanding the language of the Ofsted framework. In-service sessions are focused on all teaching and support staff securing a strong grasp of the difference between Ofsted's 'good' and 'outstanding', whether in relation to teaching, pupils' learning behaviours or leadership at all levels?

Further, senior leaders in schools try to 'climb inside the inspector's skin'. Leaders seek to share with all staff how the inspection process works, with inspectors trained to focus on students' learning and progress rather than making judgements just about teaching.

Of course, confident leaders know that an Ofsted inspection is a passing event, albeit that its verdict is important to the school community. Day in and day out, the restless schools accept no substitute for an evidence-based approach to what is happening in classrooms. Senior staff are not able to engage in anecdotal talk about say, the under-performing science co-ordinator or Head of Design and Technology, because the senior team has clear and systematic evidence, rooted in regular lesson observations and teachers' own self-evaluations, on how all staff are performing in classrooms.

In these thriving contexts headteachers place great store by how well they create 'a sense of urgency at the right time' and a shared 'it's never too late' mentality amongst all staff. Headteachers recognise that not everything can be achieved at the same time, but that staff can 'shift gear' for a sustained period of time if there is that collective ambition to improve the school. Leaders at all levels believe that if change is worth introducing, why wait until a convenient point in the calendar, say the start of the following term? If pupils' experiences can be improved sooner, then the school should change its practices without delay. This is not a recipe for undue haste, but for accelerating change when change is required.

Equally, senior leaders and governors believe strongly in a 'no surprises' culture, and thus the importance of well embedded systems that alert staff if pupils are at risk of under-achieving and under-attaining. Complementing the finely-tuned organisational systems across the school is an open, trusting culture, one within which staff know that success is applauded, and failure is supported rather than inviting blame.

In addition, leaders are very focused on eliminating 'in-school variation', or at least reaching a point where this has been reduced to an absolute minimum. One headteacher still striving for the school to be judged 'outstanding' made his mantra for the academic year: 'Let's all have a good year at the same time'.

Headteachers insist that communication of the highest quality, modelled by senior leaders, is at the heart of a high performing institution. Such communication is always anticipating staff's and students' interests and concerns, so that the school is not side-tracked by rumour, gossip and unnecessary anxiety. There is an unequivocal sense that a 'we' not 'I' culture prevails. Leaders set out genuinely to see the best in people and dwell on the positive, while at the same time being single-minded in rooting out mediocrity.

Tightening and loosening

There are, in my view, two final and telling characteristics of the successful, restless school.

Firstly, the best schools 'tighten up' to be good, but 'loosen' to become outstanding. They recognise the importance of high levels of quality control to secure good provision, evolving into higher levels of quality assurance. Thus a whole-school culture of excellence is created, within which teachers and students alike feel empowered to take measured risks.

In the end, what are schools about but what happens in class-rooms? It is the accomplished, freed teacher, comfortable in her own knowledge of subject matter, who is able to master and manage high quality digression. To watch creative intellectual digression which builds on pupils' previous knowledge and dares them to think differently – whether in the early years outdoor learning area or in an A Level chemistry seminar – is to witness fine learning.

Second, the successful, restless school is fundamentally 'outward-facing'. Significant numbers of staff work on external agendas, sometimes linked to training school status, sometimes linked to federations and primary-secondary clusters. These schools enjoy partnerships with other schools and education providers: their staff are constantly bringing back good ideas into their own classrooms from external sources.

And a key aspect of this outward-facing philosophy is the way in which the schools cite the value of 'external critical friends' who are invited from time to time to see the school 'with a fresh pair of eyes'. These friends validate changes, champion great practice and point out where there is still scope for development.

Successful schools and their leaders are restless. There is a strange paradox at their core: they are very secure in their systems, values and successes yet simultaneously seeking to change and improve. These schools look inwards to secure wise development; they look outwards to seize innovation which they can shape to their own ends and, importantly, make a difference to the children and students they serve.

REFLECTIONS
REFLECTIONS

1. From your experiences of schools which you have visited and taught in, what do you think makes up the cocktail of very good schools?

2. What good practice have you seen with schools (departments, faculties, sections, teams) keeping themselves under constant review, which leads to improvements?

3. What in your view makes for effective leadership, at all levels, in schools?

4. What are the merits of the argument outlined above about 'outward-facing' schools?

5. What do you understand, in the context of both schools and individual classrooms, about the notion of 'tightening and loosening'?

13

Recommended books on schools and teaching, and articles by Roy Blatchford

Recommended reading

Adcock, J (1994) *In Place of Schools.* London: New Education Press.
A radical, short volume on how schools will no longer exist by the mid twenty-first century. The book challenges our ideas of what 'classrooms of the future' might look like.

Barber, M (1996) *The Learning Game: Arguments for an education revolution.* London: Gollancz.
This book shaped Prime Minister Tony Blair's 'Education Education Education' agenda – written by its chief architect.

Benn, M (2011) *School Wars.* London: Verso.
One of the most readable accounts of what is happening in education today, with the coming of the Academy and Free School movement. The author believes strongly that the comprehensive school ideal is being lost.

Benson, A C (1902) *The Schoolmaster.* New York and London: G Putnam's Sons.
Written by a master at Eton at the start of the twentieth century, what it has to say about the classroom is as true today as it was then: pupils don't change!

Blatchford, R (2011) *Sparkling Classrooms.* Winsford: AMS Educational/ NET.
The author's attempt to capture the essence of great classrooms around the world, based on over 8000 lesson observations in all kinds of schools.

Carr, J L (2003) *The Harpole Report.* Bury St Edmunds: Quince Tree Press.
A fictional, amusing history of a primary school, seen through the eyes of the beleaguered headteacher. Lots of delightful episodes, ideal for reading in assembly.

Chubb, J E and Moe, T M (1990) *Politics, Markets and America's Schools.* Washington, DC: Brookings Institution Press.
A provocative, seminal work which threw down the gauntlet to governments in America and beyond: should the state provide education or should it be left to the market?

Dunford, J (1998) *Her Majesty's Inspectorate of Schools since 1944.* London: Woburn Press.
Inspection has played a vital part in how schools and teaching have

developed. John Dunford records this with wit and an eye for the right historical detail.

Gardner, H (2008) *Five Minds for the Future.* Boston, MA: Harvard Business School Press.

Much known for his work on multiple intelligences, Gardner defines here what he believes to be are the essential kinds of minds required for twentieth century teachers and pupils.

Hargreaves, D (1982) *The Challenge for the Comprehensive School.* London: Routledge and Kegan Paul.

For those interested in the evolution of the comprehensive school in this country, this is a must-read, and beautifully written with plenty of anecdote.

McCourt, F (2005) *Teacher Man.* New York: Scribner.

A brilliant account of teaching in New York classrooms, full of urban myths, pathos and humour.

McKinsey & Company (2007) *How the world's best-performing school systems come out on top.* Available at: www.mckinsey.com

A much-quoted text identifying the key characteristics of school systems globally which are performing very well today. The book has some telling observations on the vital importance of great teachers.

Phinn, G (1996) *Classroom Creatures.* Doncaster: Roselea Publications.

A collection of short poems – ideal for reading aloud in class – which capture the fun and fundamentals of classroom practice.

Robinson, S (2012) *School and School System Leadership.* London: Continuum.

An excellent and authoritative account of school leadership over the past two decades, and what this has meant for headteachers and teachers.

Smith, J (2000) *The Learning Game.* London: Little, Brown and Company.

Written by a life-long teacher, in common with A.C. Benson's book above, there are not many teacher autobiographies that better this one. Short and highly readable.

Winkley, D (2002) *Handsworth Revolution.* London: Giles de la Mare Publishers.

One headteacher's true account of transforming a large inner-city primary school, set against political and social events of the latter part of the twentieth century.

Willingham, D (2009) *Why Don't Students Like School?* San Francisco, CA: Jossey Bass.

The book (by an American writer) poses a series of challenging questions about why pupils may not succeed at school, and seeks to present some answers, some not altogether orthodox.

Are we, at last, all agreed that 'satisfactory' is just not good enough?
Roy Blatchford

Ofsted have just closed the consultation period on the new inspection framework, due to start in January 2012. For many schools this summer and autumn, they will be part of the pilots for the new framework.

Ofsted will celebrate its twentieth birthday in 2012. When established in 1992, Professor Sutherland, its first chief inspector (part-time you may recall), wrote in his Annual Report that 'the intention of, and even the justification for, Ofsted's existence is to make a contribution, through these inspections, to raising standards and improving the quality of educational experience and provision.'

Has Ofsted succeeded?

I recently returned from inspecting schools in the Middle East, to a *nine* point inspection framework. A school awarded grade 8 or 9 is threatened with closure. There are three kinds of 'satisfactory'! What is certain is that within a short space of time, this nine point scale will shrink to five, or fewer. Look at England's experience over the past twenty years.

All over the Middle East, inspection systems based on the Ofsted framework have taken root. The governments buying in international inspectors are united in one ambition: to create world-class schools in order to attract businesses and families from across the globe. Satisfactory schools for them are simply not part of the picture.

Yet in England, twenty years on from the birth of Ofsted, we have close on a third of schools described by the inspectorate as satisfactory. Too many, I would contest, are grindingly satisfactory. Some pundits call these primary and secondary schools, in all parts of the land, deeply satisfactory.

Worryingly, 40% of lessons seen by Ofsted last year were judged satisfactory.

In the face of such statistics, the recent consultation about a revised framework has focused on shrinking the number of headings under which schools will be judged. Fine as far it goes. Have fewer judgements. But the elephant in the room, the one key feature *not* consulted on, is the grading system itself.

All kinds of digressions filter into Whitehall under the umbrella aspiration to achieve world-class education. At one moment, it's copy the Swedish model of schooling; then it's follow the Finns, who have no national inspection system to speak of; then it's emulate inner urban New York and the KIPP schools.

The truth is ministers should set their stall out and say, unequivocally, that 'all English schools will be good schools within three years'. England *will* have a system on a par with the best in the Middle or Far East.

We are too late now for the 2012 Ofsted framework. But let the next edition spell out quite clearly the following criteria against which all schools and lessons taught will be judged:

- *Excellent: above standard expected – grade 1*
- *Good: standard expected – grade 2*
- *Improvement required: below standard expected – grade 3*

Quite simply, let us agree that satisfactory is not good enough. All head-teachers and governors tell you this, but the current system allows school leaders who receive a satisfactory judgement to breathe a sigh of relief. Ofsted commits itself to monitoring and revisiting a percentage of these schools, but still too many of the nation's children languish for a school lifetime in mediocre provision.

Educational inequality narrowed in the past decade, and let it be acknowl-edged that Ofsted has played its part. That said, 'satisfactory' schools are still concentrated disproportionately in the most deprived parts of the country.

Two thirds of children from the highest socioeconomic groups get five GCSEs at grade C+, but only a third of those from lower socioeconomic groups do the same. That number falls to a fifth for pupils on free school meals. Alan Milburn, the government's social mobility adviser, is fond of describing this educational apartheid. Under a *Times* headline of 'For a

British Obama we need better schools', Milburn went as far as to comment: 'This not just a social injustice. It is a moral outrage and must change.'

As Ofsted approaches its twentieth birthday, the time has come for it to play its vital part in challenging the assumption that 'satisfactory is good enough'. It plainly isn't, and particularly for those children in our schools who most need good and great teaching to transform their life-chances.

Just maybe, the soon-to-be-appointed new Her Majesty's Chief Inspector of Schools in England will run with this baton. No better year in which to do it than 2012: Ofsted's twentieth birthday and Queen Elizabeth's Diamond Jubilee.

(Article first published June 2011, at www.mikebakereducation.co.uk)

Reading: the golden key
Roy Blatchford

Provisional figures for 2011 indicate that, in England, one child in five reaches age 11 unable to read confidently. Confident, that is, to access the secondary school curriculum they are embarking on this month. History suggests that those same children will struggle over five years of secondary schooling to achieve an English grade C at 16+. The latest GCSE tables indicate that thirty per cent of 2011's cohort of sixteen year olds failed to achieve that benchmark.

What is it in our wealthy nation, with its long history of free education, that we perpetuate such failure in reading: the golden key to accessing the rest of the school curriculum and a lifetime's opportunities?

The great linguist Noam Chomsky identified that every human has an innate language acquisition device. Only in rare circumstances do humans not learn to speak, and this is true across cultures. The equally distinguished psychologist Steven Pinker remarked that while children are wired for sound, print is an optional accessory that must be painstakingly bolted on.

I began my working life in education in HM Prison Brixton. All educators should spend time in the education department of one of Her Majesty's prisons. It is a poignant reminder that basic literacy is a birthright that should be denied nobody.

In my days at the National Literacy Trust, I used to give talks entitled 'Have you ever met a mugger who's read *Middlemarch*?' This was my way of affirming that whatever else we do for children and young people in classrooms, we must give them the dignity of being able to speak, read and write with fluency to make their way in the endlessly fascinating global society which they inhabit.

So what's to do?

Neil Kinnock, Labour party leader in the 1980s, once said that the word 'priority' should not be used in the plural. Asking a school not to set out a number of priorities at the start of a new academic year would be a vanity. But let me challenge every primary and secondary school in the land to put reading as its number one priority for 2011–2012. We must break this cycle of a sizeable part of the young population growing up with stuttering language skills. Let us be properly ambitious.

- *Every primary should say to itself: all children will at age 11+ have a reading age which matches at least their chronological age.*
- *Every secondary should say that, no matter the child's starting point, they will achieve at least a grade C in English at 16+.*

First, schools need a rigorous approach to word recognition: enabling children to use a phonetic approach, to divide words into syllables for pronunciation, to have a knowledge of prefixes and suffixes.

Second, a planned approach to vocabulary development: learning new words, keywords and concepts, technical abbreviations and etymology, symbols and formulae, through regular and consistent use of a dictionary and a thesaurus.

Third, a systematic engagement with comprehension and organisation of text: summarising what has been read, distinguishing essential from nonessential, fact from opinion, drawing inferences and conclusions, noting cause and effect, reading between the lines.

Fourth, a programme to promote reading interests: voluntary reading for pleasure, reading for personal information, developing a passion for particular subjects, the use of the school and public library, the downloading onto the iPad of a favourite biography.

Fifth, a whole-school-every-teacher knowledge of study skills: sitting still long enough to read, using skimming for different purposes, reading maps and graphs, learning how to take notes, reading more rapidly with adequate comprehension, forming the study habit.

In recent years I have taught reading to Year 2 children, using the enchanting picture-books of Anthony Browne to develop a first understanding of inference. I have taught able Year 6 children to appreciate the beguiling narrative of Harper Lee. I have coached Year 10 students in GCSE comprehension exercises.

Reflecting on the five points above, skilled teachers will not make the mistake of adopting simply an age-related approach to the teaching of reading. Rather, they will select what works for a given child or group of children at a particular point in time. They will be driven by the belief that every child will leave their hands able to tackle texts with confidence, whether on the printed page or the Amazon Kindle.

Let us make this a true Year of Reading, measured in an outcome that condemns no child to a life of fractured literacy.

(*Article first published September 2011, at www.mikebakereducation. co.uk*)

Appendix: Teachers' Standards Posters

1 Teachers' Standards Poster: Myths and Facts (pp84–5)

2 Teachers' Standards Poster: How will they be used? (pp86–7)

3 Teachers' Standards Poster (pp 88–9)

Posters issued to schools in 2012 by the DfE.

Teachers' Standards
Myths and Facts

Myth: Schools can keep their existing Performance Management policies because the new Appraisal Regulations are permissive and do not require anything new.

Fact: Although in general the new Appraisal Regulations allow schools much more flexibility than the 2006 Performance Management regulations, they have introduced one new requirement.

In future, teachers' performance must be assessed against the Teachers' Standards. Appraisal policies that do not provide for assessment of performance against the Teachers' Standards will not comply with the 2012 Appraisal Regulations.

Myth: The Teachers' Standards apply only to teachers in maintained schools

Fact: Academies and independent schools will not have to assess their teachers' performance against Part One of the Teachers' Standards as part of an annual appraisal process. If they take part in statutory induction arrangements, they will, however, have to assess NQTs against the Standards at the end of their induction period.

Part Two of the Teachers' Standards applies to all teachers, including those in academies and independent schools.

Myth: There are three new Career Stages for teachers: "NQT", "mid-career teachers" and "more experienced practitioners"

Fact: These are not rigid career stages, but examples of different levels of experience that teachers might have. Teachers' performance should be assessed against the Teachers' Standards to a level that is consistent with what should reasonably be expected of a teacher, given their current role and their level of experience. Schools will naturally have higher expectations of their experienced teachers than they will of their NQTs.

Myth: Schools should adopt a model which exemplifies the Teachers' Standards for teachers at different levels of experience

Fact: The independent review group considered and rejected the suggestion that expectations should be defined for teachers at different career stages.

The government agrees that it is not necessary or helpful for schools to adopt rigid models that seek to set out exactly what the Teachers' Standards mean for teachers at different points on the pay scale. Head teachers and others should use their professional judgement and common sense when appraising teachers' performance against the Teachers' Standards.

Myth: Head teachers and other members of the Leadership group should not be assessed against the Teachers' Standards

Fact: Head teachers, Deputies and Assistant Heads are covered by the Appraisal Regulations and also need to be assessed against the Teachers' Standards. Appraisers should use their common sense when assessing performance against the Standards.

Myth: Post-Threshold, Excellent Teachers and ASTs should not be assessed against the Teachers' Standards

Fact: As part of the annual appraisal process, the performance of post-Threshold, ETs and ASTs in maintained schools must be assessed against the Teachers' Standards. Schools can, if they wish, also assess these teachers against relevant higher standards.

In addition, any teacher applying for assessment against higher standards will first be assessed against the Teachers' Standards.

Myth: The Teachers' Standards cannot be used to assess the performance of QTLS teachers

Fact: It is up to schools to decide which standards they wish to use to when assessing the performance of QTLS teachers. There is no requirement for schools to assess QTLS teachers' performance against the Teachers' Standards, but they can do so if they wish.

Myth: The Threshold, Advanced Skills and Excellent Teacher pay grades are being abolished and replaced with Master Teachers

Fact: The Teachers' Standards Review Group recommended in its second report that the existing standards for Post-Threshold, Excellent Teacher and Advanced Skills Teacher should be discontinued, and that a new Master Teacher Standard should be introduced.

The Secretary of State welcomed this recommendation in principle, but the School Teachers' Review Body will need to advise on the future of these existing pay grades. No decision has yet been taken and the current post-Threshold, ET and AST standards will continue as they are for the time being.

Myth: Teachers' performance will be assessed against the Teachers' Standards from 1 September 2012

Fact: Although the Appraisal Regulations come into force on 1 September 2012, most teachers' next appraisals are likely to take place under the 2006 performance management regulations, because those regulations continue to apply in relation to any performance management cycle already in progress on 1 September 2012.

From September 2012, any teacher applying for assessment against higher standards will first be assessed against the Teachers' Standards.

The Teachers' Standards can be found on the DfE website: www.education.gov.uk/publications

Teachers' Standards
How will they be used?

"A relentless focus on high-quality teachers and teaching requires a clear and universal understanding of the basic elements of good teaching. The standards which define our expectations for teachers' professional practice should therefore set the benchmark for excellent teaching and exemplary personal conduct. They should set a standard to which all trainees aspire, and which all qualified teachers adhere to and improve upon throughout the various stages of their career."

Sally Coates, Chair of the independent Teachers' Standards Review and Principal of Burlington Danes Academy.

What are the Teachers' Standards?

- The Teachers' Standards set a clear baseline of expectations for the professional practice and conduct of teachers and define the minimum level of practice expected of all teachers in England.

- They were developed by an independent review group made up of leading teachers, head teachers and other experts.

"The new Teachers' Standards give an unequivocal message that highly effective teaching is what matters in this profession. The Review Group has seized the opportunity to raise the bar for current and future teachers. Our nation's children and young people deserve no less."

Roy Blatchford, Deputy Chair of the independent Teachers' Standards Review and Director of the National Education Trust

Those involved in training and inducting new teachers will use the Teachers' Standards to ensure quality of new entrants to the profession

- The Teachers' Standards will be used by Initial Teacher Training (ITT) providers to assess when trainees can be recommended for Qualified Teacher Status.

- They will be used by schools to assess the extent to which Newly-Qualified Teachers can demonstrate their competence at the end of their Induction period.

Practising teachers will use the Teachers' Standards to support their own professional development and growth

- They can be used by individual teachers to review their practice and inform their plans for continuing professional development.

- The most successful education systems in the world are characterised by high levels of lesson observation. Teachers benefit from observing each others' practice in the classroom. Teachers learn best from other professionals. Observing teaching and being observed, and having the opportunity to plan, prepare, reflect and teach with other teachers can help to improve the quality of teaching.

- Many teachers are keen to improve their own practice by having feedback on their own practice from colleagues and from observing the practice of others.

Head teachers and other school leaders will use the Teachers' Standards to improve teachers' quality, by setting minimum expectations of teaching in their schools

- The Teachers' Standards will be used by maintained schools to assess teachers' performance and help schools and teachers to identify development needs and plan professional development.

- Head teachers (or other appraisers) are expected to assess teachers to a level that is consistent with what should reasonably be expected of a teacher given their role and their level of experience.

- They will also be used to ensure that teachers meet minimum standards if they apply for assessment against higher standards (post-Threshold, AST and ET).

The Teaching Agency will use the Teachers' Standards when hearing cases of serious misconduct

- Since April 2012, Part Two of the Teachers' Standards can be used by the Teaching Agency when hearing cases of serious misconduct, regardless of the setting where a teacher works.

"[The Teachers' Standards] set clear expectations about the skills that every teacher in our schools should demonstrate. They will make a significant improvement to teaching by ensuring teachers can focus on the skills that matter most."
Michael Gove, Secretary of State for Education launching the Teachers' Standards in July 2011

The Teachers' Standards can be found on the DfE website: www.education.gov.uk/publications

Teachers' Standards

PREAMBLE

Teachers make the education of their pupils their first concern, and are accountable for achieving the highest possible standards in work and conduct. Teachers act with honesty and integrity; have strong subject knowledge, keep their knowledge and skills as teachers up to date and are self-critical; forge positive professional relationships; and work with parents in the best interests of their pupils.

PART ONE: TEACHING

A teacher must:

1 Set high expectations which inspire, motivate and challenge pupils

- establish a safe and stimulating environment for pupils, rooted in mutual respect
- set goals that stretch and challenge pupils of all backgrounds, abilities and dispositions
- demonstrate consistently the positive attitudes, values and behaviour which are expected of pupils.

2 Promote good progress and outcomes by pupils

- be accountable for pupils' attainment, progress and outcomes
- be aware of pupils' capabilities and their prior knowledge, and plan teaching to build on these
- guide pupils to reflect on the progress they have made and their emerging needs
- demonstrate knowledge and understanding of how pupils learn and how this impacts on teaching
- encourage pupils to take a responsible and conscientious attitude to their own work and study.

3 Demonstrate good subject and curriculum knowledge

- have a secure knowledge of the relevant subject(s) and curriculum areas, foster and maintain pupils' interest in the subject, and address misunderstandings

6 Make accurate and productive use of assessment

- know and understand how to assess the relevant subject and curriculum areas, including statutory assessment requirements
- make use of formative and summative assessment to secure pupils' progress
- use relevant data to monitor progress, set targets, and plan subsequent lessons
- give pupils regular feedback, both orally and through accurate marking, and encourage pupils to respond to the feedback.

7 Manage behaviour effectively to ensure a good and safe learning environment

- have clear rules and routines for behaviour in classrooms, and take responsibility for promoting good and courteous behaviour both in classrooms and around the school, in accordance with the school's behaviour policy
- have high expectations of behaviour, and establish a framework for discipline with a range of strategies, using praise, sanctions and rewards consistently and fairly
- manage classes effectively, using approaches which are appropriate to pupils' needs in order to involve and motivate them
- maintain good relationships with pupils, exercise appropriate authority, and act decisively when necessary.

8 Fulfil wider professional responsibilities

- make a positive contribution to the wider life and ethos of the school

- demonstrate a critical understanding of developments in the subject and curriculum areas, and promote the value of scholarship
- demonstrate an understanding of and take responsibility for promoting high standards of literacy, articulacy and the correct use of standard English, whatever the teacher's specialist subject
- if teaching early reading, demonstrate a clear understanding of systematic synthetic phonics
- if teaching early mathematics, demonstrate a clear understanding of appropriate teaching strategies.

4 Plan and teach well structured lessons

- impart knowledge and develop understanding through effective use of lesson time
- promote a love of learning and children's intellectual curiosity
- set homework and plan other out-of-class activities to consolidate and extend the knowledge and understanding pupils have acquired
- reflect systematically on the effectiveness of lessons and approaches to teaching
- contribute to the design and provision of an engaging curriculum within the relevant subject area(s).

5 Adapt teaching to respond to the strengths and needs of all pupils

- know when and how to differentiate appropriately, using approaches which enable pupils to be taught effectively
- have a secure understanding of how a range of factors can inhibit pupils' ability to learn, and how best to overcome these
- demonstrate an awareness of the physical, social and intellectual development of children, and know how to adapt teaching to support pupils' education at different stages of development
- have a clear understanding of the needs of all pupils, including those with special educational needs; those of high ability; those with English as an additional language; those with disabilities; and be able to use and evaluate distinctive teaching approaches to engage and support them.

- develop effective professional relationships with colleagues, knowing how and when to draw on advice and specialist support
- deploy support staff effectively
- take responsibility for improving teaching through appropriate professional development, responding to advice and feedback from colleagues
- communicate effectively with parents with regard to pupils' achievements and well-being.

PART TWO: PERSONAL AND PROFESSIONAL CONDUCT

A teacher is expected to demonstrate consistently high standards of personal and professional conduct. The following statements define the behaviour and attitudes which set the required standard for conduct throughout a teacher's career.

- Teachers uphold public trust in the profession and maintain high standards of ethics and behaviour, within and outside school, by:
  o treating pupils with dignity, building relationships rooted in mutual respect, and at all times observing proper boundaries appropriate to a teacher's professional position
  o having regard for the need to safeguard pupils' well-being, in accordance with statutory provisions
  o showing tolerance of and respect for the rights of others
  o not undermining fundamental British values, including democracy, the rule of law, individual liberty and mutual respect, and tolerance of those with different faiths and beliefs
  o ensuring that personal beliefs are not expressed in ways which exploit pupils' vulnerability or might lead them to break the law.
- Teachers must have proper and professional regard for the ethos, policies and practices of the school in which they teach, and maintain high standards in their own attendance and punctuality.
- Teachers must have an understanding of, and always act within, the statutory frameworks which set out their professional duties and responsibilities.

The Teachers' Standards can be found on the DfE website: www.education.gov.uk/publications

References

Department for Education (2011a) *First Report of the Independent Review of Teachers' Standards: QTS and core standards.* London: DfE. Available at: www.education.gov.uk

Department for Education (2011b) *Second Report of the Independent Review of Teachers' Standards: Post-threshold, excellent teacher and advanced skills teacher standards.* London: DfE. Available at: www.education.gov.uk

Department for Education (2012a) *Teachers' Standards*. London: DfE. Available at: www.education.gov.uk

Department for Education (2012b) *School Teachers' Pay and Conditions Document 2012*. London: DfE (1 September 2012). Available at www.education.gov.uk

General Medical Council (2012) *Good Medical Practice*. Available at: www.gmc-uk.org

Ofsted (2012a) *School Inspection Handbook*. London: Ofsted. Available at: www.ofsted.gov.uk

Ofsted (2012b) *The Framework for School Inspection*. London: Ofsted (5 September 2012). Available at: www.ofsted.gov.uk

Rutter, M, Maughan, B, Mortimore, P and Ouston, J, with Smith, A (1979) *Fifteen Thousand Hours: Secondary Schools and Their Effects on Children.* London: Open Books.

Index